SHELLEY W

How I Changed MY LIFE

- in -

A Year!

One Woman's Mission To Lose Weight, Get Fit,
Beat Her Demons, And Find Happiness
In Twelve Easy Steps!

ZANDER

Livonia, Michigan

Published by BHC Press

Library of Congress Control Number: 2018931004

ISBN: 978-1-947727-46-5 (Softcover)
ISBN: 978-1-947727-98-4 (Ebook)

Visit the publisher:
www.bhcpress.com

How I Changed MY LIFE

- in -

A Year!

One Woman's Mission To Lose Weight, Get Fit,
Beat Her Demons, And Find Happiness
In Twelve Easy Steps!

Books by Shelley Wilson

Nonfiction
Motivate Me!
How I Changed My Life in a Year
How I Motivated Myself to Succeed
Meditation for Children

Teen Fiction
Oath Breaker
Oath Keeper
Guardians of the Dead
Guardians of the Sky
Guardians of the Lost Lands

THE Monthly CHALLENGES

I dedicate this book to the loving memory of my cousin, Lee.

His smile lives on in all of us.

INTRODUCTION

SO MUCH can happen in 365 days but how many of those days do we squander away?

Take a moment to think about something you've always wanted to do, have or learn. If you'd started working towards it twelve months ago it could be yours now.

As a holistic health practitioner it's my job to help my clients control their anxieties and limiting beliefs, and work towards their own goals with confidence. I draw on my own life experiences to show people that anything is possible if you just believe in yourself.

Ten years ago I walked away from an abusive marriage, taking my three very small children with me. I started over—new home, new schools and a new job.

I went to night school to retrain in holistic therapies while working during the day as a sales manager in a conference and event department. I gradually built up my client list until I could leave my sales role and start my own holistic business.

Recently my eldest son said to me, 'I'm so proud of you, Mum. Even when you're really tired you still get up and carry on.'

As thoughtful and lovely as that was, I didn't want my children to be proud of me for simply existing on a day-to-day basis. I wanted to show them that they could achieve anything when they set their minds to it, but how would I show them?

As yet another year rolled to a close I decided that if I was going to show my children—and my clients—that it was possible to make your dreams come true, then I'd have to prove it.

Sitting at my parents' house on New Year's Eve, I realised that my string of broken New Year's resolutions would be the best starting point. Regurgitated goals swam around my brain; get fit, read more, lose weight—all respectable objectives until you eat your own body weight in leftover mince pies before the decorations come down! Resolutions abandoned.

I CHALLENGED myself to stick fastidiously to completing twelve resolutions, one a month, over the next year. To add to the pressure I decided to blog the results for the world to see: *www.motivatemenow.co.uk*

When I began the challenge I had clear objectives, to teach my children they can achieve their wildest dreams and to show my clients that they are amazing women who can empower themselves to accomplish their own ambitions. I wanted to motivate people with the challenges I set myself. Never did I expect it to change my life.

This book is designed to be a motivational tool to help you rekindle forgotten passions or make changes which are long overdue.

If you fancy starting your own resolution challenge, don't feel you need to wait for New Year's Eve. Start today, start on Monday, or begin at the start of a new academic year. Don't put that dream on hold anymore—do it today. In just 52 weeks you could be prolific in Italian, running your own business, relocating to the seaside or editing your first novel.

Month 1
LOSE WEIGHT

"I am healthy and happy in my own skin."

DO YOU know what the number one resolution has been for the past few years? If you'd said 'weight loss' then you'd be wrong—it's actually 'to read more'.

As I never have a problem with switching off the telly and curling up with a good book I chose to begin my challenge with the second favourite resolution, to lose weight.

My weight loss challenge couldn't have come at a better time, I'd had to invest in larger work trousers to accommodate my expanding waistline, I had four boobs instead of two and I hated to admit it...I had back fat.

My goal for month one was to start a healthy eating regime (I don't like the word *diet*). It takes 21 days to break a habit so I hoped that by day 22 I would be able to look a bag of crisps in the eye and say quite confidently, 'Not today thank you.'

So where to begin?

I could follow one of the many weight loss plans published in magazines or I could go online but I knew if I wasn't kept in check I would cheat and 'forget' that I ate a deep-fried Mars bar after lunch.

There was only one weight loss programme which would work for me and that involved physically attending meetings and interacting with people. So I joined Weight Watchers.

They have an excellent e-source system which would, combined with the weekly meetings and standing on those scales in front of another person, keep me motivated.

Let the weight loss begin...

BY WEEK two I was still recovering from the shock of my first weigh-in at my meeting. I was astounded to find that I had put on two stone in just seven months; this I discovered as I teetered on the scales, stripped down to the bare minimum of acceptable attire for a council library annexe room.

My Weight Watchers' leader, Andrea, looked at me sympathetically as she handed me a smiley face sticker. 'All the support you need is here,' she told me.

Lesson one was how to clear out cupboards and the fridge to rid ourselves of temptation. I closed my eyes to conjure up a picture of my fridge: beer, wine, potato salad, pasta, chocolate and a bottle of milk. I was going to be in so much trouble.

'Clear it out—everything has to go.' Andrea told us how we could get crafty with our leftovers such as freezing cheese in small chunks, sending chocolates to our neighbours and moving any other temptations out of sight.

After an hour of clearing my kitchen I got rid of the following:

Cheese: *wrapped and in the freezer.*

Pasta salad: *kids had it for lunch.*

Beer: *donated to my grateful dad.*

Wine: *that stayed put because you just never know when you'll have a bad day!*

I ordered my shopping online so I couldn't be tempted by special offers on high-calorie snacks and I even bought crisps for the kids in a flavour I don't like so I wouldn't be tempted.

The contents of my fridge were now healthy options such as vegetables, fruits and yogurts. It looked like a rainbow had exploded in there.

AS WEEK three arrived the weather turned icy so I managed to leave my frost-covered car and walk my daughter to school nearly every day. The exercise and fresh air helped with the weight loss.

Even though I had a great start to my weight loss, losing six pounds in three weeks, my willpower flagged at the weekend, and on one occasion I did succumb to a treat on a Saturday night; the children were in bed so I had sole control of the television (a rare treat in my house), and I foolishly decided to watch *Beaches* while dealing with an array of turbulent emotions (I put it down to those nasty Christmas toxins coming out of my system).

Weepy film + emotional woman = sob fest.

It wasn't pretty and yes, I attacked the crisp cupboard. Granted I only devoured the one pack (cheese and crackers and a chocolate bar) but I felt awful. On Sunday morning I looked like I'd had an allergic reaction to something, and my face was swollen and puffy. I was determined not to let my moment of weakness trip me up so I spent the day cooking up a batch of bolognese, vegetable soup and a lamb casserole for the freezer. I felt so much better and even though my vegetable soup (free points) looked a bit like wallpaper paste, it tasted fabulous.

Week three is the most notorious for abandoning our New Year's resolutions and I could relate to this.

To make myself feel better I cleared the drive of all snow, which obviously deserved a treat—this then turned into two treats when it started snowing again and my freshly cleared drive had yet another blanket of snow over it.

I refused to let this minor setback veer me off course, so, for the *third* time that week I drew a line under it and started again, Until my

parents turned up to take the four of us off for hot chocolate and crois-
sants. SNOW DAYS ARE FATAL.

It's not rocket science; all I needed to do was 'Eat Less' and 'Move
More'. Surely even my brain could understand that concept?

Weight Watchers to the rescue again; according to their new plan
there IS a scientific reason why I can't stop shovelling snacks as well
as snow.

We all understand that when we haven't eaten for a while and our
stomach is empty, we encounter a physical urge to eat (homeostatic
hunger). Scientists have now discovered that we also have a physiolog-
ical urge to eat which can make us believe we are hungry when it's not
real hunger (hedonic hunger). Both ways activate the same area of our
brain. Weight Watchers helps members to form positive eating habits
to control the hedonic urge to eat.

So it would appear that I was not the failure I believed I was, but
my willpower was being tested. With two days until my next weigh-in—
could I turn it around in time? The tension mounted, it was nail-biting
stuff (note to self—check how many *Propoints* in chewed fingernails).
I was aiming for another pound loss but if I managed to stay the same
that would be a mini triumph in my toughest week yet.

Of course it didn't help when I got text messages from Domino's
checking if I was okay because they hadn't heard from me in a while!

I LOVE Rhonda Byrne's book *The Secret* and have Mike Doolan's
inspirational quote, '*Thoughts become things, pick good ones*' written on a
chalkboard in my kitchen.

When my children are having an off day and all I hear is 'I can't
do this homework...' or 'I'll never remember my spellings...' I take
great pride in tapping my chalkboard and showing them my 'Mummy
knows best' face.

I therefore had to laugh when I was sat at my kitchen table, head
in hands at the prospect of my imminent weigh-in, moaning at myself

for being a reckless snack-eating freak, and my 15-year-old son tapped on the board as he walked past and raised his eyebrows in a look beyond his years.

I narrowly missed his head with the tea towel as he ran off laughing—cheeky sod.

He did perk me up though, so I wrapped up warm, pulled on my Wellington boots and trudged through the snowdrifts to my meeting.

I'm so glad I did as I had lost another one and a half pounds.

I had spent all week blaming the snow for my lack of motivation to eat healthily and yet because of the bad weather, I had abandoned my car under five feet of snow and walked everywhere.

Our quest for the week ahead was to take control of our 'snack attacks' when watching TV. I had scoured the cupboards and removed anything with 'chocolate' or 'Pringles' in the title, leaving me with sugar-free jelly, meringue nests, Weight Watchers yogurts and lots of fruit.

As the fluffy white stuff continued to pour from the skies I decided that this week's meal planner would have to be warming as well as filling.

A normal day for me now consisted of the following:

Breakfast: Porridge made with water or soy milk, banana and blueberries.

Snack: Fruit

Lunch: Homemade vegetable soup with a tuna salad sandwich on brown bread (no butter) and a small bunch of grapes.

Dinner: Spaghetti bolognese.

TV snack attack: Meringue nest with jelly and a Weight Watchers yogurt.

Not bad when I look at what I used to eat on an average day:

Breakfast: Two chocolate brioche rolls, cup of tea

Snack: Cup of tea and a couple of biscuits

Lunch: Cheese sandwich (on white bread and with butter), crisps, cup of tea and a biscuit (or three)

Dinner: Steak pie, chips and baked beans

TV snack attack: Tea and biscuits at every advert break.

Plus wine, takeaway pizza and chocolate at the weekends.

What a difference 31 days can make.

MY FIRST challenge of the year was to start a healthy eating regime. After joining Weight Watchers and dealing with the shock of my current weight, I spent month one cooking up a storm, menu planning and making better choices. This meant I entered month two ten pounds lighter.

I weighed less, had lost inches from my wobbly bits, had more energy and found the social aspect of attending Weight Watchers meetings invaluable.

Month one had made me re-evaluate what we, as a family, put in our bodies, and the harm processed foods, fats and sugars can do. Going to my weekly meetings offered the support I needed to keep going, stay motivated and have a really good laugh. If you want to do a healthy eating plan but can't get to a slimming group, find a friend who will be a 'diet buddy', weigh in together at home and keep each other going. Support is key.

I'd had a few wobbles on the way this month, most of those fuelled by chocolate cravings and emotional outbursts. I'd had moments of madness, such as eyeing up the kids' pet goldfish and fantasising about him deep-fried with a pile of chips.

I'd tried to resist alcohol, but sometimes that glass of Chardonnay was the only thing that would de-stress me. I'd experimented with over 20 new recipes and the kids had supported me through the highs (chicken pie) and the lows (chilli con carne) without so much as a 'P-l-e-a-s-e can we just have chips tonight?' and 'Who knew sweet potatoes were so yummy?'

Month One = Mission Completed

Month 2
GET FIT

"I am creating my best me, one step at a time."

TO 'GET Fit' in one month would be an impossible task after 40+ years living a sedentary lifestyle. I was delusional if I thought I could breathe and walk simultaneously let alone achieve fitness. Moving the goalposts slightly, I changed this resolution to 'Move More'.

Did you know the absolute minimum amount of exercise we should all be doing is half an hour, five days a week? I hadn't done that since I was six, so I decided that that was going to be my minimum target—should be easy enough.

As I cast my mind back 30 years, I had fond memories of me and my school pals skipping across the daisy-filled playing fields, pigtails swaying in the balmy summer breeze, singing along to the skipping rope song of the week 'Ally, ally, up-see-daisy...'

Let's fast forward to the present day; now a 42-year-old, sedentary, mother-of-three, and skipping just didn't have the 'glow' I remembered.

Let me paint you the picture—it was a miserable day outside but I was eager to get started on the 'Move More' part of my resolution. I decided that due to the fact I had no ceiling pendants I could get away with skipping indoors. After taking out the wall light fitting, I moved to the front room which was slightly bigger.

I cleared a space and flicked on the telly to keep me company.

Any warm, fuzzy feelings about skipping soon fizzled out when I started leaping around my living room. I resembled a lava lamp—folds of flab clashing together, boobs bouncing right and left, up and down.

Top Tips to consider before embarking on a skipping regime—

- wear a sports bra
- and Tena Lady
- knee supports, elbow pads and a crash helmet wouldn't go amiss either.

After five minutes I had turned an alarming shade of crimson and my heart was singing to me,

'What—are—you—doing?

You—crazy—fool?

What—are—you—doing?

You—crazy—fool?'

If I tried to do half an hour of this, my kids would be mopping my remains off the lounge carpet.

So, for the sake of my children, I stopped after seven excruciating minutes and spent the next twenty-three flat on my back watching the tiny, tweeting birds, circling about my head.

I decided to adopt a triathlon style to my routine and hopefully it would keep me from keeling over. I would do five minutes of skipping, five minutes running up and down the stairs and five minutes of wall slides/squats. This was still challenging but not so suicidal. My heart was now singing,

'Skip—Jog—S l i d e,

Skip—Jog—S l i d e'

I was glad when the week was over; I found skipping much tougher than I had expected but all that lava-lamping meant another pound lost at Weight Watchers. Not all bad then.

WE ALL learn to walk at a young age, so you would think that walking is as natural as breathing but apparently I wasn't doing either right.

Swinging my hips was a no-no, panting and gasping for breath—another no-no, causing embarrassment to my daughter—the biggest no-no of them all. So I stopped swinging my hips as I walked her up to school and tried to relax into a brisk pace as I embarked on a week of walking.

It does help to have a lovely place to walk: a forest, the park or a canal path, but the main road at rush hour didn't have the same aura about it, and my coughing and spluttering added to the look of desperation, but at least I was out and moving more.

Women normally walk at 3 mph as an average, but if you want to lose weight then you need to walk a bit faster. 4-6 mph will help you cover a mile in 10-15 minutes and contribute to your weight loss. It's great if, like me, you are 5 feet 10 inches, but when I went walking with my mum who is 5 feet 3 inches, she was practically sprinting alongside. Do what feels comfortable for you.

There are some excellent books and websites, such as *www. verywellfit.com* offering tips and advice on walking for weight loss and health.

Don't forget you can get the family involved: walk the dog (or someone else's), walk to school or work instead of taking the car, park at the car park farthest away from the shops.

As I discovered, walking hadn't just helped my weight loss, (another pound) it also lifted my mood. There are emotional benefits to walking—increased energy, less stress, better sleep and it can relieve your PMS.

Alongside the emotionally upbeat feelings, you also reduce the risk of heart disease, stroke, type 2 diabetes, high cholesterol, and a whole host of other nasties. It's got to be worth throwing on a good pair of trainers or walking boots and popping out for a stroll.

WHEN I decided on a 'Move More' resolution I wanted to embark upon a treasure trove of exercises from my youth, which is how I ended up skipping, hula hooping and walking—all very old school.

By week eight I was feeling inspired to crank up the volume, get down with the kids and bang on the Wii Fit. Oh yes, if it was good enough for the youngsters then it was good enough for me.

In my 'oh so distant' youth I could throw a few decent shapes on the dance floor. Of course those amazing dance moves were carefully choreographed in my bedroom with my Wham LP blasting from my record player—yes, I said record player!

However, today's kids are lethal and they take no prisoners. My son is a prime example and happens to be awesome on 'Just Dance'.

Let me quickly explain the rules for those of you without a Wii, without this particular game, without kids, or simply for all those sensible people out there. You can choose from a huge range of songs, from the more up-to-date rap songs to Elvis. Once selected, a dancer pops up on the screen (or multiple dancers if you are challenging an opponent) and it's your task to follow what they do as if dancing in a mirror. When they go left, you go left, when they jump up and down, you jump up and down, fairly straightforward—you would think.

Our first challenge was a song from The Blues Brothers. I was happily singing along, thinking how lovely it was to be having fun with my children, when I got a smack in the eye from my son's Wii remote as I failed to duck, swing and s-l-i-d-e in time to the music. Fun? I was black and blue by the end of song three.

To save my delicate skin from bruising like a peach, I decided to abandon the dance game and switch to the Wii Fit, a relaxing fitness regime I could enjoy on my own. I was pretty bad at the baseball and absolutely rubbish at bowling but I thoroughly enjoyed the boxing. Word of warning though—I felt like I had done ten rounds with Mike Tyson the next morning; my arms and shoulders ached like crazy but I do believe the old bingo wings weren't quite so flabby.

AS WEEK nine approached I decided to slow things down slightly and take some inspiration from my dad who is an avid cyclist. Now I'm no Tessie Reynolds and had absolutely no intention of recreating her Brighton-London-Brighton trip on a bicycle. I was, however, very grateful that, at the young age of 16, Tessie had taken on her momentous task, causing a national scandal in the process, and allowing me the freedom to wear my joggers to tackle my exercise bike instead of petticoats, bloomers and fluffy skirts.

My dad has been a cyclist since before I was a twinkle in his eye. He's a really good one too, training four times a week and covering around 200 miles. He still races during the summer and even manages to stay on two wheels on occasion (he will forgive me that quip as I am, more often than not, the one who collects him from the various hospitals dotted across Warwickshire, if he takes a tumble).

I, however, did not follow in his footsteps (or wheel spokes) in the fitness department. Height, dark colouring and dry wit are all I managed to inherit.

So when I informed him I was going to be including a bike in my fitness regime he fell about laughing. Not easily deterred, I popped up to Argos and bought an exercise bike—okay, so I may not feel the wind in my hair, the flies in my teeth or the cow shit under my fingernails but I would be moving more and that's what month two was all about.

Don't get me wrong, cycling is fantastic exercise and when my family went on holiday a couple of years ago, we all enjoyed biking through the amazing landscapes, but for this challenge I decided a stationary bike would be easier for me to manage. In other words, I would be a liability if let loose on the roads.

Exercise bikes are a wonderful way to have a cardio workout; they are low impact and easy on the ankles, knees and joints. After running a half-marathon a couple of years ago, my knees took a hammering, so I was grateful for anything with 'low impact' on the box.

I hadn't managed my dad's 200 miles (not even close), but at least I was moving. I was strengthening and toning my legs and my gluteal muscles and getting ever nearer to looking like Angelina Jolie.

Using the exercise bike did have its uses. As I was inside I could catch up on any TV I had recorded, belt out my Bon Jovi album and wheel spin to 'Livin' on a Prayer' or get stuck into a good read, all while toning my lower body.

It's hard work this exercise thing but why can't we have fun along the way too, that's what I say.

Month Two = Mission Completed

Month 3
DO SOMETHING CREATIVE
Stop Procrastinating

"I am creative and happy to share my talents."

CREATIVITY IS different for everyone. My talented friend Sarah knits the most amazing cardigans and jumpers. My son creates stunning pastel and oil paintings for his art coursework. My mum makes her own handmade cards and my good friend Nicki can knock up a quilt in a weekend! Check out Nicki's website:

www.sunshinegirlnicola.blogspot.co.uk

All of these crafts are wonderful ways to flex your creative muscles. For me, it's writing that ignites my creative side. Writing stories inevitably came from my passion for reading. As soon as I learnt to read I was hooked; I was a walking sponge with pigtails!

My favourite book as a child was Enid Blyton's *The Folk of the Faraway Tree* and I still have my original copy some 30 plus years later.

When I wasn't reading, I was writing short stories and little poems about the seagulls outside my bedroom window. At the tender age of fifteen I had my exam coursework—a children's picture book—read out in class; a proud moment. I have written a number of manuscripts but like the hundreds of other wannabe writers, my stories have gathered dust in a desk drawer.

As I got older I picked up my pen once more and had another stab at it, this time concentrating on magazines. I was published in my local newspaper, in *Fate & Fortune, Slimming World Magazine, Your Home, Writing Magazine, Woman Family Health Special, Scrapbooking, Spirit & Destiny* and spent six months as a reader agony aunt for a feature called 'What's your problem?' in *Woman*.

Yet again life took over and I laid my pen down to rest with the usual self-doubting thoughts swirling through my mind, 'not enough time' and 'not good enough'.

So on New Year's Eve I decided that enough was enough, I needed to stop procrastinating and just get on with it—I had to Make Time!

"You will never win if you never begin."

~ Helen Rowland ~

The question then was, how to get the creativity flowing? I made a list—I love making lists so this was the fun part—action steps, if you like, of how to make time in my daily schedule to write and how to keep up with the momentum.

1. I joined a creative writing night class through my local college.

2. I submitted short stories and flash fiction to five writing competitions.

3. I wrote book reviews on Amazon and GoodReads.

4. I managed to achieve something I thought was impossible—I wrote every single day! That included blog posts, stories, a business newsletter, letters to magazines and my creative writing class homework and I realised the 'not enough time' was a lie; if you love something enough you'll *make* the time and I suddenly realised how simple it was.

By week eleven I was in the full swing of my creative challenge and loving every second of it, but I also had to keep up with the day job. That of course got me thinking about how I could use my work to inspire my creativity challenge.

One of the workshops I run is a vision board course. This two-hour workshop helps my clients to create a vision of what they want in their lives from career, love, family, or health matters.

When I was thinking about characters and scene setting for my creative writing class it dawned on me that vision boards could help in creating stories too.

I went through a pile of magazines and cut out any photographs or pictures I felt a connection with; in other words, pictures that made me smile.

Feel free to give this exercise a go, it really is addictive and you could end up with a long list of story, poem or article ideas—no more writer's block! If you don't want to write a bestseller then use the instructions below to create a vision of what you want in your life: collect pictures of sports cars, happy people, piles of money, people exercising, pictures that represent the job you want or ideal man (I have a whole board dedicated to Johnny Depp.)

All you need to get started is the following:

1. A cork board or other suitable base (a scrapbook works just as well)

2. Large assortment of magazines (choose magazines that you wouldn't normally pick up)

3. Glue and scissors

That's it; you are ready to go.

1. Flick through the magazines and tear out ALL the photographs, wording, pictures and sayings you see which draw your eye or make you smile. Don't question why you like these things, just cut them out and start to make a pile.

2. Once you have a good selection, spread them out in front of you and begin to lay your favourites on the board. Some of your original choices may not feel right anymore, just put those to one side for now.

3. As you lay your pictures out you may start to feel the story coming together; it's helpful to have a notepad handy so you can make notes.

4. When your board is covered, take a good look at what you have created. Is there a bestselling novel planned out before you? If you can't feel it yet then put it away for a couple of days.

I make a vision board every New Year and fill it with all the things I hope to achieve in the coming year; hanging it up where you see it every day affirms your wishes and helps you to action them.

You can create vision boards for anything: the life you desire, job you dream about, health, creative stories, or you can make one as a gift for a wedding or special birthday.

This is how I came up with my twelve resolutions on New Year's Eve. Being creative is so much fun and vision boards are a wonderful pastime. Kids love to make them too.

If you're going to get creative then you've got to have some fun; as actor John Cleese once said, 'If you want creative workers, give them enough time to play.'

Getting creative doesn't need to involve a pad and pen, artist's easel or a pair of knitting needles. In fact you may only need a bath full of cold beans or running shoes and an Epilepsy Research UK T-shirt!

By week twelve I was taking my 'Do Something Creative' resolution in a different direction.

Question: If you were asked to raise money for your favourite charity, what creative ideas could you come up with?

Here are a few of my favourite ideas...

- Dress up in fancy dress at work or school
- Have a bake sale
- Sponsored walk, swim or car wash
- Shave your head! (Okay, this one may be a bit drastic but it certainly worked for Jessie J on Comic Relief)

WHEN I lost my 24-year-old cousin, Lee, in December 2010 to SUDEP (Sudden Unexplained Death from Epilepsy), our family and friends began a campaign to raise awareness and funds for Epilepsy Research UK. My aunt and uncle started the 'Lee's Smile' charity at an amazing gala ball held at Elland Road football stadium in Leeds, hosted by the wonderful Liz Green from BBC Radio Leeds, where we raised a massive £80,000 ($106,000 USD).

Lee was such an amazing athlete and this prompted many of us to get involved in sporting events: the Great Manchester North Run, Rotary Stratford Half-Marathon, a sponsored swim, football and cricket events and the Three Peaks Challenge. On top of this we'd had coffee mornings, ladies' lunches and fashion shows. My children's junior school even dedicated an entire week to fundraising for Epilepsy Research UK and raised £2175 ($2884 USD).

By being creative with fundraising it helps to raise much-needed awareness for your chosen charity.

Aside from the funds and awareness, one of the other benefits of being as creative as you can be is the chance that it could lead somewhere amazing. Take Cassidy Megan, for instance. She founded Purple Day back in 2008 after struggling with her own epilepsy; she is a young girl who had a big creative dream. In 2009 her creativity went international when the New York-based Anita Kaufmann Foundation and The Epilepsy Association of Nova Scotia joined her campaign.

On March 26th we are all encouraged to wear purple for epilepsy awareness.

For our fundraising efforts we were given an opportunity of a lifetime. To help celebrate Epilepsy Research UK's 20th anniversary in 2012, we were invited to No. 10 Downing Street. YES, I said No. 10, home of the prime minister! What an amazing day that was.

So if you fancy doing the Hugh Grant (Love Actually) dance down the corridor of No. 10—yes I actually did that—or drinking the PM's wine, then get your creative head on and think up some fabulous ways to fundraise for your chosen charity, and if you don't have a favourite then please feel free to join us at 'Lee's Smile.'

www.leessmile.com

To finish off my creative month I had a 'doodle fest' using the American Zentangle method. This is a creative art form where all you need is paper, pencil and a pen.

Don't panic if you can't draw or paint, if you've never used acrylics or pastels or if you think a canvas is something you sleep under—which of course it is but that's for another book!

A couple of years ago I discovered this creative art form which is not only simple to do, even for a non-drawer, but also therapeutic and meditative (huge tick in the box for my holistic alter ego).

Cast your mind back to your school days for a moment. Were your school books covered in little doodles? Spider webs drawn across your maths book; eyes, bubbles and snakes sketched on the homework diary and, of course, the occasional love heart—complete with initials—on your French textbook.

We all 'doodle', whether it's on school books, drawing a moustache on Simon Cowell's picture in a magazine, or on the gas bill as you wait in the phone queue— *'You are TENTH in the line, your call is important to us...'* —doodle, doodle, doodle and suddenly your love hearts have horns and breathe fire!

I am a regular visitor to the Hobbycrafts show at the National Exhibition Centre in Birmingham and I met the inspirational Alison Thompson from Old Hall Crafts on one of my visits.

She was the woman responsible for my addiction to Zentangling. Of course this particular addiction has helped me to become better at meditation and calm any anxieties that crop up day-to-day.

My children love to 'tangle' and my daughter's friends often create amazing little projects when they come for a sleepover.

So what on earth is Zentangle?

Zentangle was created by Rick Roberts and Maria Thomas. Maria was working on background patterns for a manuscript and mentioned to Rick what a feel-good experience it was and how she was able to focus without thought or worry as she worked. Rick realised she was describing the feeling you achieve during meditation. They put their heads together and hey, presto.

Don't worry if you can't even draw a straight line, this could be the creative pursuit for you. There is no right or wrong way. In fact, if you did 'go wrong' then chances are you've just invented a new 'tangle' pattern.

There are some wonderful videos on YouTube to help you create fantastic patterns or for inspiration.

I would recommend logging on to the Zentangle website for top tips and amazing designs and ideas; Rick and Maria's blog is a wonderful read and you can also subscribe to their newsletter and be kept up-to-date on Zentangle news and events. Links can be found at the end of the book.

You may wonder why I bother spending time zentangling but I can say it has helped me on many occasions.

- **Insomnia:** We've all had sleepless night for one reason or another. Having a blank notepad and a pen by the bed means I can tangle for a while, calming my thoughts and drift easily back to sleep.

- **Sausage & mash moments:** The ladies on my meditation classes understand all about Sausage & Mash moments. You are drifting into a meditative state, concentrating on your breathing then—wham! 'Did I put the cat out?', 'Have I locked the back door?', 'Shall we have sausage and mash for tea?'

Zentangling helps you to concentrate on being in the moment and allows you to leave your sausage & mash moments for later—reducing stress and anxiety and improving your focus.

You don't have to keep your new-found creative talents to yourself either. Frame a tangle, make cards or bookmarks. You can even tangle on furniture, MDF (medium-density fibreboard, an engineered wood product which can be cut into letters/words) and fabric to enjoy at home.

Here's how to get started:

Tangles can be drawn on anything, but traditional tangles are drawn on 'tiles' (3 1/2" x 3 1/2" smooth art paper square).

1. Draw a dot in each corner with a pencil, about 5mm from the edge.
2. Join the dots. Don't worry if your line is wobbly, it adds to the uniqueness.
3. Draw a zigzag, a loop or a swirl across the centre
4. Using a pen (Micron is recommended) draw tangle patterns (doodles) in each section.
5. Simple as that.

If you would like to see some of my creations you can find my post dedicated to Zentangle at:

www.myresolutionchallenge.blogspot.co.uk/2013/03/art-at-tack-resolutions-get-crafty-with.html

There are many books available as well as the online resources (links can be found at the end of the book) to find tangle patterns but look around you, at your wallpaper, the pattern on your socks, even the tread on your trainers; they all make perfect tangle patterns to use on your art.

By the end of week 13 my creativity was bouncing off the walls: I had entered more writing competitions, signed up for another fun run for charity and made some Zentangle gifts for presents.

Month Three = Mission Completed

I would like to express my thanks to Rick and Maria for giving me permission to share their wonderful creation with my readers. Please do stop by their site and say hello.

NB: 'Zentangle', 'the red square', and 'Anything is possible, one stroke at a time' are registered trademarks of Zentangle, Inc.

Month 4
GIVE UP THE DEMON DRINK

"I am in control of my own well-being."

MOST PEOPLE enjoy a tipple or two. You may enjoy catching up with colleagues in the pub after work on Thursday, or your Friday night curry just wouldn't be the same without a couple of beers. The pub lunch with the girls on Saturday is crying out for a glass or two of Chardonnay and no Sunday roast would be complete without a nice Rioja.

It is far too easy to include alcohol in our lives and before we know it we are drinking above the Government's recommendations.

I do enjoy a drink or three and not wanting to come across as a raving alcoholic I decided to do a spot of research for my alcohol-free resolution. The results were shocking...

So what are the Government guidelines?

The Government advises that we *do not* regularly drink *more than* the daily unit guidelines: for men this would be three to four units a day. This is the equivalent of a pint and a half of four per cent beer a day. For women it's less, two to three units which is the equivalent of a 175ml glass of wine.

If, like me, you have fabricated the number of units you consume when asked by your doctor—go on, admit it—then you need to log on to the Drinkaware website. This site is a wonderful resource for all your alcohol-related questions. (Links can be found at the end of the book.)

They have a simple calculator where you can work out your units per day or week. It calculates the total number of units, total number of calories and shows you just how much damage you are doing to your health. I was shocked to discover that after a 'jolly' Easter Sunday spent with my family, I was classified as a 'binge level drinker'.

Okay, I admit we did consume a fair amount over our Easter buffet and I was a peculiar shade of green on Bank Holiday Monday, but binge level? Maybe this no-alcohol resolution wouldn't be such a bad idea after all.

My April resolution was therefore under way, 30 days alcohol-free, no alcohol, *où est le vin*? This was going to be a tough one. I could have chosen February to tackle this resolution as it would have been a shorter month but I was here now, the challenge had been set and I was ready and raring to go.

Luckily for me I am a bit of a 'tea-face' so when I looked at my wine-free fridge at least I knew I could put the kettle on and have a nice cup of Tetley instead. However, I had planned a week away with my children, my Dad's birthday party and a girl's night out, all without so much as a sip of alcohol—moral support would be needed.

Heading down the M5 to spend our Easter break at the Haven Holiday Village, Burnham-on-Sea would normally be a cause for celebration. On this occasion I had a sense of trepidation; could I enjoy my holiday without alcohol?

Yet again I appear to be giving you all the impression that I am some half-soaked mother who is permanently attached to a bottle of gin. I assure you this is not the case—I prefer vodka!

Holidays go hand in hand with relaxing by the pool, watching a good turn at the clubhouse and enjoying a meal out at a local restaurant. Staying on a site with everything you could possibly need on your doorstep means you can leave the car and let your hair down—or enjoy a latte in the coffee lounge if you are off the demon drink.

SO MY mission for week 15—surrounded by clinking glasses and merry holidaymakers—was to work my way through the soft drink menu; lemonade, diet coke and a hideous slushy which left my tongue blue.

Normally, when the kids go swimming and hit the water slides, I park myself in the bar overlooking the pool with a good book and a large glass of *vino* (me time is a rare luxury.) Glancing around at the frosted beer glasses I chose to climb into my swimsuit and join the children before stopping off for a hot chocolate with extra whipped cream on the way back to the caravan. *Note to self—don't tell my Weight Watchers leader just how many hot chocolates I had.*

Is it possible to enjoy a holiday without alcohol? Well, yes it is and it happened to be much easier than I thought.

If you have an alcohol-free month coming up on your own resolution list then my three top tips may help you plan:

Offer to drive to local attractions to put paid to the temptation for a lunchtime drink.

Check out the drinks menu for non-alcoholic alternatives; many holiday centres offer great mocktails.

Treat yourself to a new top, manicure or iTunes download if you manage one week alcohol-free.

If you don't think you fancy going cold turkey on holiday then pace yourself on a night out and alternate alcoholic drinks with soft ones. You can find lots of top tips at *www.drinkiq.com*.

Burnham-on-Sea Holiday Village holds many happy memories for us as a family. Aside from the lovely food, proximity to the beach and the variety of attractions, it is also the place where I won a dance competition several years ago. I'm sure you are now picturing me in a beautiful ballgown or high heels and a saucy salsa number—

sorry to disappoint, this particular dance contest was for the Cha Cha Slide! One balmy summer evening I was adopted by a Welsh family who believed they were saving me from my sad, singleton evening as I nursed a bottle of wine while my children danced and played with new-found friends; it all went downhill from there!

As it happens my kids were very proud of their mum, since I beat the other contestants on the stage and won—yep, a bottle of wine!

Would I be able to replicate this stardom without the Dutch courage of a glass or two of Rioja?

It occurred to me, as I stood under the spotlight in the centre of the brightly coloured Big Top at Paulo's Circus, that it has nothing to do with alcohol; I just have one of those faces that means every entertainment rep or 'clown' finds it incredibly easy to drag me up onstage, make me do stupid things and send me on my way. Of course, following on from my unexpected five minutes of fame with Paulo's Circus I had a craving for circus-related mocktails.

Luckily I had a few blog readers who accommodated me with some lovely recipes:

'Flying Fairbrother' from Tracey Mason

In a shaker half-filled with ice, combine 2oz grapefruit juice, 1oz orange juice, 1oz cranberry juice and 1 tsp of honey. Shake well. Strain into a Collins glass almost filled with ice cubes and top with 3oz ginger beer. Stir well and enjoy.

'Lion Tamer' from Brenda Wilson

Cut a small watermelon into chunks and freeze overnight. When fully frozen, blend with two and a half cups of almond milk in a blender until smooth. Pour into a glass and garnish with sprigs of mint and enjoy.

'Coco the Clown' from Amanda Thomas

Drizzle some fudge sauce around the rim of a martini glass. Blend 2oz chocolate ice cream, one can of coconut cream and crushed ice for two minutes in a blender until smooth. Pour into the prepared glass and enjoy.

Week 17 and the fourth week alcohol-free was a tough one. I'd been asked by every one of my clients at work, 'How are you coping without alcohol?' I obviously have a reputation!

My answer surprised me. I was miserable. Never did I imagine that giving up alcohol would be so hard. I've had three children and was able to abstain from drinking while pregnant and for many months after giving birth each time, I gave up for a year in 2010 after having a bout of low self-esteem. So why had I found this particular challenge so tough?

This got me thinking about cravings and how it might be possible that the 'stuff' between my ears, commonly known as the brain, may be the culprit. I was right, and during my research I discovered that alcohol cravings are linked to low blood sugar; this therefore explains why I had been stuffing my face with four Wispa bars a week.

The part of our brain which is affected by addiction is also the same part which allows you to exercise willpower—no hope for me, then! Heavy alcohol intake can cause changes to our brain which then takes a while to return to normal. The advice handed down from the professionals suggests changing your habits and mental association with alcohol. This makes sense as I often find myself pouring a glass of wine at 6 p.m. on a Friday from habit.

If this sounds familiar then why not try to retrain your mind and body? Instead of pouring a glass of wine, put the kettle on. If you always have a bottle with a Chinese, order a pizza and make a jug of squash. By doing something different you are altering your brain's associations and making it easier to cut down on your alcohol intake.

Try it out for yourself or see what other habits you can change; I always have a blueberry muffin when I go to Costa out of habit—there lies my next challenge.

As I trawled the web looking for like-minded souls, I came across Tara Gladden's Wonder Women blog at The *Telegraph*. She gave up drinking in January to support Cancer Research UK and her Diary of a Dryathlete is definitely worth a read.

Would I do it again? Yes I would, but I think giving something up for a good cause, as Tara did, gives you a reason and therefore tricks the grey matter into thinking it's a good idea.

If you are planning to give up drinking, whether it's for charity, financial, health and weight loss reasons, or you just want to cut back, then the Internet is full of useful information. The Drinkaware site is a marvellous resource and for those with a more serious addiction Alcoholics Anonymous has a refreshingly helpful website. (Links can be found at the back of the book.)

Month Four = Mission Completed

Month 5
DO SOMETHING I'VE NEVER DONE BEFORE

"I am adventurous."

AS TEMPTED as I was to break open the bubbly and celebrate the end of my alcohol-free month, I refrained so I had a clear head for the start of my May resolution challenge.

'Do Something I've Never Done Before.'

When I originally wrote my challenge list I selfishly included things I knew I would enjoy (it is *my* list after all!) even if I knew they would push me in some way.

On paper it was fairly straightforward. I had a *very* long bucket list and all I needed to do was to choose my four favourite challenges, but the universe had other ideas and suddenly my best-laid plans were up in the air. I couldn't complain though as the additional challenge which presented itself to me was definitely something I'd never done before.

An opportunity arose to talk about my job in a bid to help an entire junior school year group and so I jumped at the chance. I love working with children, I love my job and as anyone who knows me will confirm, I love to talk!

That is how I ended up running my first Stress-Busting Workshop for year six at my local junior school.

As my own daughter was struggling to cope with the anxiety of sitting her SATs, I felt a responsibility to these children who, aged just ten and eleven, were coping with an ever-changing world, a mix of emotions and anxieties, and raging hormones which they were struggling to understand.

Out of all the self-help techniques I offer my clients, I decided to use Emotional Freedom Technique (EFT) with the children and based my entire talk on 'tapping', to help release their fears, anger and worries prior to their tests. With a move to secondary school also on the horizon we covered their feelings towards this.

Emotional Freedom Technique (EFT) is a simple energy therapy which enables you to free yourself from emotional negativity. Our body operates in harmony with our energy system and when this energy is disrupted we experience blocks. Any imbalance in the body's energy system can have profound effects on our personal psychology. A distressing memory causes a negative emotion and this in turn can manifest as a physical illness.

Its founder, Gary Craig, recognised that tapping on the end points of the body's energy meridians was effective in relieving these blocks and releasing negative emotions and memories which may have plagued us for years.

Deep-rooted issues are always best handled with the support of a qualified EFT practitioner and you can find a local therapist through the AAMET website. (Links can be found at the end of the book.)

Children take to this therapy very quickly and I therefore knew that my presentation would need to be quick and fun so I didn't lose my audience. I included a variety of exercises and tied this in with relevant key stage curriculum links to enhance their learning. I introduced my bear, Ray, who was happy to have stickers attached to him to show the tapping points.

It was a huge success and the children were amazing. They got involved with the practical side of the workshop and volunteered where necessary. When I asked them to suggest emotions we could work on, they provided me with a variety of feelings, including being stressed, bored, nervous, scared and even excited. They were a credit to their school and a pleasure to work with.

Running through the presentation prior to their arrival, in a bid to ensure I didn't let the children down, I had rehearsed and rehearsed the slides so much that the practice tapping I did on myself totally chilled me out and I was able to thoroughly enjoy the experience. What an incredible way to start my 'Do Something I've Never Done Before' challenge.

I do love to plan and organise and I am an avid list maker, but the one lesson I have learnt during my resolution challenge is to be wide open to opportunities as some of them could just change your life.

Once I came down from the euphoria of helping others I had to tackle the rest of my list of challenges. I say 'challenge' in the loosest sense, as the activities I took part in couldn't really be classed as challenging—except maybe for the zip wire!

Could I top teaching year six at my local junior school on how to survive anxiety caused by exams? Well, no, probably not but then unique opportunities should never be overlooked.

That got me thinking about my lovely clients who patiently pore over my blog posts and listen to me waffle on during their holistic sessions and so I thought I'd include something new that was accessible for my readers to try and something I'd wanted to do since I was a child…make my own fairy garden.

We have always had fairies at the bottom of our garden so it was fairly apt that on a sunny bank holiday weekend, my daughter and I set about making a fairy garden.

I dug (no pun intended) about in the shed and came across an old wine crate which was the perfect size for our little fairies and then we went into creative mode:

1. We assembled our tools: the crate (any small container will do—remember to drill drainage holes in the bottom), our compost, plants and, of course, the fairies!

2. We filled the crate with a black bin bag so the wood didn't rot and then added a layer of stones to help with the drainage. When this was done we emptied the compost on top and smoothed it out.

3. Once the compost was in place we were able plant our flowers; we used some small stones to mark a path through the garden (so the fairies didn't get their shoes dirty) and added a solar lamp (available at any garden centre or supermarket). Well, fairies do like to play out at night! We chose mixed lobelia as they are easy to grow and would give us a colourful garden for the summer.

4. With all of our flowers planted up we then invited our fairies along and they all seemed delighted with their new garden! Don't worry if you haven't got any fairies to hand—sprinkle your garden with a little fairy dust and they will find you!

So there you have it, a perfect fairy garden. Great for any garden or patio area and don't worry if you don't have a garden, why not have a go at making one in a plant pot? With some leftover plants and a selection of crystals, my daughter made a smaller garden in a little plant pot that was going spare—perfect for a window ledge. If you want to take a look at the fairy garden we produced, follow the link on my blog:

www.myresolutionchallenge.blogspot.co.uk/2013/05/four-simple-steps-to-create-your.html

I began to realise that having a go at something new didn't mean I had to break a world record or reinvent the wheel. This challenge had certainly made me think outside the box, but I'd also realised that it was the little things that counted just as much as the life-changing achievements.

I spent a wonderful weekend with my daughter and seeing the smile on her face when we watered our little garden and watched the solar light flicker on at dusk was simply priceless. 'Do Something I've Never Done Before' really had been my favourite challenge so far.

As I hit week 20 I realised how much I was looking forward to ticking off the next challenge on my list. It never occurred to me on New Year's Eve that I was going to have so much fun doing such basic things and making such simple changes.

And week 20's challenge was as simple and basic as it got because I'm NOT a sewing guru, in fact I was most definitely a virgin when it came to all things needle and thread, and sewing did come under my 'Do Something I've Never Done Before' banner.

First of all I must say a huge thank you to Nicki from Sunshine Reflections who was my 'Yoda' for this challenge. She patiently talked me through the process, offering her expert advice and a calming word when the sewing machine freaked me out. Nicki's blog has some of the amazing projects she has done. (Links can be found at the end of the book.)

So, as a quilting newbie I opted to make a cushion cover rather than a king-sized bedspread (phew!) and in an 'Idiot's Guide' fashion here's how I got on:

1. I chose my pattern: a simple 15" cushion cover with 9 x 5" squares. The pattern I picked had a star in the centre so five of the squares were broken up into sections of the star.

2. I chose my fabric and feeling patriotic I opted for a truly British theme of red, white and blue.

3. I traced the pattern shapes onto paper and cut them out. *Top Tip—If you think you will re-use your pattern cut-outs, laminate them so they last.*

4. Using a large cutting board and a very nifty rotary cutter (a special tool to cut material) I cut out the fabric using my templates.

5. Once all my pieces were cut out, I laid them out to double-check before I started sewing. (There were four x 5" corner pieces, the other five sections were made up of triangle slices, the very centre square had four sections—two x red and two x blue—and the four outer sections had two x flag pattern and one coloured triangle.)

6. Next step was to pin the sections together; we did this two little bits at a time so I only had to sew small sections to begin with. I did one row at a time until I had three strips of 15" x 5".

7. Once that was done I sewed the strips together (carefully) until I had a finished front panel.

8. With my 'awesome' front section completed we chose two fabrics to make up the back side, one x 9" and one x 12". These would overlap to form the envelope to keep our cushion filling safe. I did a hem along one edge of each piece so they looked neat and then it was time to put it all together.

9. Turning the fabric so it was pattern side facing each other, I sewed the front and back pieces together and

did a reverse stitch over the seam ends for added strength.

10. Once I had gone all the way round it was time to turn the cover the right way round and see the finished product...my first ever handmade quilt cushion cover and no blood, sweat or tears.

My 'Do Something I've Never Done Before' month was going very well, however, I seemed to have the knack of fitting extracurricular activities into the schedule. Week 21 was supposed to be the perfect time to calm my antics slightly and enjoy a girlie pamper session— definitely something I've never done before as I am such a tomboy— but prior to my lash-tastic hour of bliss I was faced with the daunting task of putting together a mountain of flat-pack furniture.

Allow me to explain. My daughter went away with school for a week and I thought that would be the perfect opportunity to redecorate her bedroom as a surprise. At the time it didn't cross my mind just how much work this would entail but as the cardboard boxes kept arriving my stress levels began to peak. The 14 packages included a corner wardrobe, a triple wardrobe, a double wardrobe, a bedside cabinet, a desk and a single ottoman bed.

Flat-packs can be a challenge at the best of times but with just three days to build, paint and dress the room I realised I had bitten off a little more than I could chew.

It was one of my lovely clients, Lynda, who suggested that I use this experience as part of my challenge and blog about the details. 'How often do you flat-pack?' she asked. So true. So my speedy room makeover became part of my resolution challenge.

I must say I felt a huge sense of satisfaction when it was finished and my daughter squealed with delight when she got home. My hands were covered in blisters, my knees were creaking in a most alarming manner and every inch of my body ached but this challenge was definitely worth the blood, sweat and tears.

SO FINALLY, after the last of the empty boxes had been recycled, I could concentrate on my original plan and enjoy a girlie pamper session with Ellie from Solihull based 'Beauty by Ellie'.

I reclined on the spa couch and turned my stunted little lashes over to a very talented beautician. It wasn't what I expected—in fact I would highly recommend eyelash extensions purely for the relaxation of it. I would have nodded off if my good friend Sarah hadn't been primed as star photographer and kept prodding me for my next shot.

It was pain-free, quick and relaxing and I found it highly amusing when Ellie brushed my new long lashes with her tiny lash comb.

I may be female but I am most definitely not a girlie girl. As a child I was often found up a tree or on a rope swing and my tomboy ways extended into my adult life where I am happier in jeans and Converse rather than dresses and high heels. So, doing something so ladylike was most definitely a challenge, but I loved my long luscious lashes—there may be hope for this tomboy yet.

AS WEEK 22 arrived so did the sunshine, together with the grand finale for May's challenge, 'Do Something I've Never Done Before'.

When I decided on New Year's Eve, to do these challenges I had the basic idea in place. It had evolved over the months but I knew there were certain goals I had put off over the years and this challenge would be the motivation I needed to see them through.

Writing, creative pursuits, weight loss—all respectable goals, but I wanted to show my clients and my children that it doesn't hurt to think outside the box.

Never at any point did it cross my mind that screaming my lungs out as I plummeted through the trees, lassoed to a strip of wire would appear on my To Do list!

OUR FAMILY holiday to Center Parcs in the beautiful Sherwood Forest Village in Nottinghamshire was pre-booked ready for the half term holiday and so, as I perused the activities brochure I had a moment of madness and thought, *'Oh what a great idea! I'll add an action challenge to my blog.'*

So that is how 'Zip Wire' appeared on the list.

I thought it would be fairly easy as I'd done abseiling, kayaking, pot-holing and rock climbing. I'd also been to the top of the Eiffel Tower, Empire State Building and World Trade Centre. What I failed to realise is that I was eleven when I tackled those adventurous activities and in my teens and twenties when I travelled.

It was only as I stood in a full harness and safety helmet that I remembered I was 42, a single mother of three and bloody petrified!

My eldest son very kindly accompanied me on this 'trip of terror' and I was very grateful to have him by my side. My hands started shaking the second I walked through the gate. The staff were fantastic and went through the health and safety regulations clearly and explained the course to me in idiot-proof language, as I think they realised I was a wee bit nervous.

The time came to climb up the ladders to reach the walkways. Lee went first and I followed behind with an army of eight-year-olds bringing up the rear (I'm not joking—I was the only adult and the only one trembling.)

I honestly thought I would be sick as I stepped out onto the tiny wire bridge. All that kept going through my mind was 'I'm a Celebrity Get Me Out of Here' and I half expected Ant and Dec to meet me at the end! Luckily the day was dry and sunny. I can't even imagine what it must be like crossing that first bridge in the rain. My palms were sweating so much I was struggling to cling on as it was.

Finally, bridge one was complete. My legs were shaking so much and my head was pounding from the concentration. Lee was steaming ahead and I could hear the excited giggles of the kids behind me

(probably wondering if they would get into trouble if they threw the old bird off the bridge who was holding up their fun!)

Bridge number two loomed, this one didn't look so bad, and at least there were flat footholds. If only the thing would stop swaying I might be able to keep my breakfast down.

As I stepped onto the tiny wooden platform at the end of the bridge, I let out a rather large 'OMG,' which of course the giggling children behind thought was highly amusing. 'You'll be fine,' they said. That was easy for them to say as they probably weighed two stone altogether. Knowing I was carrying a little 'holiday weight' I had visions of the wire snapping as I launched myself off the platform and into the abyss.

The member of staff on the ground shouted some comforting words to me before adding, 'After three, just jump.'

Madness! If my heart hadn't been trying to escape my chest and my knees had been able to stop knocking I might have taken a moment to appreciate the amazing scenery. The sun filtered through the trees and the light breeze carried the sounds of chattering squirrels and the woodland birds...

For the love of God.

Then he said, 'JUMP!'

So I jumped...then screamed the whole way down.

Surprisingly I kept my eyes open all the way and managed to see the wonderful hues of greens and browns of the forest flash past. I spotted my brave son cheering me on and my parents and other children taking photos and videos (and laughing) and then I saw the cargo net at the end of the wire as it approached at breakneck speed.

My landing wasn't as ladylike as I would have liked but I was safely back on the ground—still shaking though.

Lee shot off to have another go as I let the nearest member of staff peel me out of my harness. 'Sure you don't want to have another go?' he asked.

Never again.

I am, however, incredibly proud of myself that I achieved this goal. The children made it look so easy and not one of them screamed. My dad captured my entire descent on his camera phone and I think I screamed enough for everyone.

Doing something you've never done before can provide you with the tools to have an amazing adventure. I may have been shaking for several hours after and my stomach was whirling for a while too but I wouldn't have missed it for the world. My daughter's hug as I reached the ground was worth the nerves—she was proud of her old mum and that felt great.

Month Five = Mission Completed

Month 6
ADOPT BETTER HABITS

"I am balanced in body and mind."

AS MONTH six began, the sun was shining, which helped to make everything look and feel so much brighter. Since I was still slightly traumatised by my encounter with the zip wire I was very pleased to note my next resolution was so much calmer. 'Adopt Better Habits.'

I came up with this challenge when I realised how I'd let my recycling slip, so this goal was a way to get back on track. As I gave it some extra thought I came to the conclusion that recycling my rubbish was a pretty lame topic to cover and all my readers would be nodding off before I'd managed to soak the label off an old baked bean tin.

So the decision was made—I was going to adopt better habits: my tins were stripped and ready for collection, my milk cartons were washed out and crushed and my cardboard was flat and bound for the paper truck—but... for the sanity of my blog readers, I decided to recycle in a more holistic way.

When I run my personal development workshops I often refer to space clearing which in turn helps to clear the mind. This is a great starting point for any new venture, idea or period of recovery. A clean slate if you like.

Clearing Your Clutter is one of the most effective ways to feel amazing, lighter, brighter—and very often a wee bit richer. So here are your four easy steps to achieving inner peace by clearing that clutter and recycling...

1. **Take Responsibility:** Look around you—are there piles of magazines, old books, CDs you no longer listen to (or have uploaded to your iPod)? Do you own 14 glass vases but never buy flowers? Does your wardrobe contain 'thin' clothes and 'fat' clothes and 'not in a month of Sunday am I going to wear again' clothes? If you said yes (go on admit it) then clearing the clutter is for you.

It is incredibly empowering to steam in and have a good sort out. I do this on a regular basis, normally when I feel my energy levels dip. I take a look around and may notice that the cupboard under the stairs is full of the kids' shoes, coats and other 'out of sight, out of mind' rubbish. A quick tidy up and I feel my energy levels begin to rise.

I love this Japanese proverb and have it stuck on my pin board, 'The day you decide to do, it is your lucky day.' It works on so many levels, but for the purpose of clearing clutter I can tell you I have found the odd fiver tucked away in old coats on more than one occasion.

2. **Take it Slowly:** I do everything at a hundred miles an hour but when I clear my clutter I tend to savour the moment. If you are looking around at a mountain of 'stuff', don't panic. it may look overwhelming but it doesn't have to be. You've taken responsibility, so the hard bit's over—now is the action part of the plan.

Take it one room at a time. When you look around the room you have chosen, break it down even further, take it one piece of furniture at a time. Clear a desk drawer or one shelf on the bookcase and then build up to the entire desk or a couple of other shelves.

3. **Tools to Help:** The only tools you will need are a big mug of coffee and three cardboard boxes. Label the boxes: Donate, Bin and Sell.

Donate: This is your charity box; anything that isn't broken but no longer has any place in your home could make someone else very happy and become their most prized possession—you did that, you made someone else happy, wow!

Bin: We all gather bits and bobs which have no value or reason. I recently cleared out my desk drawer and got rid of 19 pens which had run out of ink—who knows why I had put them back in my desk. On the plus side it gave me the perfect excuse to buy a new pen (I'm so easily pleased.)

Sell: If your resolutions started in January, then month six will coincide with summer and car boot season. If you started your resolution at another time of year, then take a look in your local newspaper for tabletop sales that are indoors and perfect for the winter months. If you've never done one before then give it a go; it's great for getting rid of bulky items as well as unloved ornaments, books, DVDs and clothes. My kids grow that fast I could hold a regular slot at the local car boot and just sell their cast-offs!

Top tips for car booting/table topping—take plenty of loose change, a flask and packed lunch, old carrier bags, plastic bags or sheets in case it rains, an old table (I use a paste table) and a friend.

4. **Completion:** You've done so well if you have made it this far, well done you. Now you just need to complete the process. You've signed up for a car boot, so the Sell box will be going.

You've driven to the local refuse centre and dropped off your Bin box. All that's left is to load up the car with your Charity box and deliver it to your nearest shop. DON'T leave it by the front door—DON'T leave it in the boot of your car. You've done so well, don't stop now.

Top Tip: anything you don't sell at the car boot, transfer directly into your charity box, and don't re-introduce it to your home.

There you go, clearing clutter in four easy steps. You will feel empowered and lighter for doing this. It doesn't matter how long it takes you either; making a start is a fantastic achievement and keeping the flow going brings about a wave of energy for you and your home. What a great habit to adopt.

A clutter-free home makes for a clutter-free mind and helps so many people to feel better about their environment and themselves.

AS WEEK 24 arrived I was still concentrating on my 'Adopt Better Habits' challenge and I decided to venture outdoors. Not such a good choice with the torrential rain, however it did help with the spade work for this week's resolution: to grow my own food.

Anyone who knows me will confirm my home contains NO living plants as I have a tendency to kill anything remotely green, so this challenge was going to be quite interesting.

A few years ago my dad made me a vegetable patch. He used some old timber and boxed out a part of my garden, then my eldest son and I dug over the soil in readiness for the bumper crop of salads and vegetables we were going to grow.

Fast forward three years and we have a bumper crop of weeds and quite an impressive variety too.

So this week was going to be the turning point for me to adopt a better habit. I dodged the rain and with spade in hand tackled the knee-high jungle. I turned the soil, I de-weeded and I planted the tiny specks of dust that fell from the packet labelled 'lettuce'.

I watched, I waited and then I got bored and made a cuppa. Growing your own is not the best activity for an impatient Gemini like myself. Fortunately I received an e-mail which gave me the perfect tools (no pun intended) to while away the hours.

Douglas McPherson, author of *Circus Mania*, dropped me a note to tell me all about World Juggling Day. A perfect pastime for a restless green-fingered wannabe like me. Douglas assured me that juggling was great for uniting the left and right sides of my brain, apparently.

His blog contains 15 facts about juggling—did you know that juggling can burn 280 calories an hour? There is also a How-To Guide if you want to give it a go yourself. My juggling was about as good as my gardening but it was certainly a fun activity to pass the time. (Links can be found at the end of the book.)

By the time my lettuces and potatoes were ready for harvest I was a pro juggler...well, in my head I was.

With all the fresh salad and vegetables available from our very own vegetable garden, I thought I would test myself to the limits for week 25 and go veggie for seven days.

When I was in my thirties—many years ago—I appeared in *Spirit & Destiny* magazine's Health MOT feature. I was interviewed by a naturopath, personal trainer and nutritionist. I discovered that as my blood type is A my body struggles to break down red meat and chicken, which can cause bowel toxicity. I was advised to cut out all red meat and cut down on chicken as well as have fish at least three times a week and drink eight glasses of water daily.

This was sound advice, but at the time I had three kids under five and a lousy husband. I also really do love a juicy steak, crave bacon butties and enjoy roast chicken dinners! Can you see how going vegetarian for a week was going to be tough? I needed help.

I wanted to combine my vegetarian week with my very first resolution of losing weight. I had done so well at the start of the year but as the months had rolled forward I had allowed a few bad habits to return, so this challenge would hopefully help me to get back on track with my weight loss challenge. I was therefore overjoyed to discover a great book with tips for losing weight, told in a light-hearted way (I don't like being 'told' what to eat) with plenty of veggie recipes.

I bought *How To Eat Loads and Stay Slim* by Della Galton and Peter Jones after being initially attracted by the fabulous title—who doesn't want to eat loads but keep a trim waist? Once I began reading I discovered a highly amusing mix of 'hunger science', quick cheats, psychological techniques and scrumptious recipes.

As a wannabe vegetarian it really helped me on my veggie week to see how Della could keep herself adequately fed without adding meat to her diet. She's also uber-trim so that was motivation enough to want to find out her secrets. Peter's veggie recipes are amazing—don't get me wrong, this book is for carnivores as well as herbivores, so there is plenty to keep the whole family happy.

For my male readers you also have a treat in store (aside from a svelte Della!). Peter's take on losing weight is hilarious and enlightening. I certainly never thought men suffered the same hang-ups as women but Peter tells it how it is in a true 'Yorkie bar' fashion.

The book also links to a corresponding website which was my go-to source for this week's challenge; Peter's veggie bean chilli was our Friday night special.

There is also a link to follow them on Facebook if you want tips, recipes and inspiration on the go. (Links can be found at the end of the book.)

MY YOUNGER son asked if he could join me for this challenge as he loves fish and vegetables. It was great to have him involved and we both enjoyed the colourful variety of foods that we ate. He wasn't too impressed with crab sticks but he did love the fat-free salad dressing from the book.

This week was a real surprise for me. I thought of it as a 'big' challenge—okay, maybe not as big as the zip wire—but I ended up looking forward to mealtimes, felt lighter and not as drained.

I'm going to take Della and Peter's advice and eat a more sensible and varied diet. I may not be able to cut all meat from my diet but using their tips and recipes I can integrate more fish and veggie dishes into our meal planner.

Take a look at the *How To Eat Loads and Stay Slim* website and start your own challenge today; it could be a veggie week or just a healthy eating campaign. Using the book and the site you won't go wrong.

If you want more information about the authors of *How To Eat Loads and Stay Slim* log on to their personal websites below:

www.dellagalton.co.uk
www.peterjonesauthor.com

Month Six = Mission Completed

MY SIX MONTH SUMMARY

ACCORDING TO the Oxford English Dictionary, 'to achieve' means 'to succeed in doing something by effort, skill, or courage.' What a lovely mantra for our daily lives.

Think about what you've achieved in the last six months. When I began this challenge six months ago, my initial aim was to complete at least one or two of the items on my New Year resolution list. I would be happy to lose eight pounds, I would be over the moon to run without the aid of an oxygen tank and I would be ecstatic to have one of my stories published.

I remember it so well, drinking bubbles and brainstorming ideas for an outstanding New Year...but wait, I HAD achieved those things and many more.

Just what had I achieved?

In month one I started my weight loss campaign—a clean slate with a fridge full of goodies. By month two I was ten pounds lighter but after my alcohol-free month (where I replaced wine with Wispa bars) my weight crept up again. Della Galton and Peter Jones to the rescue with their book *How to Eat Loads and Stay Slim* and month six saw me back on track and even surviving a meat-free week.

My 'Move More' campaign in month two tested my endurance levels with walking, skipping (not to be recommended if you are above a D cup) cycling and Wii Fit. I don't know about being fitter, but I certainly slept well that month.

In month three I got to unleash my creativity. I made vision boards, looked at creative ways to fundraise and of course I got to write, write and then write some more. Many of my favourite authors use the mantra, 'If you want to be a writer, you need to write'. So I did, and among the stories and letters I had published, my post about vision boards appeared in a full-page spread by the wonderfully talented Paula Williams for *Writers' Forum* magazine.

On occasion my resolutions had overlapped; month four was my alcohol-free month and as I coped with an Easter break as a teetotal holidaymaker, I found myself doing things I had never done before—which was meant to be month five's challenge. This included being dragged up onstage and wrapped in sticky tape at the circus by Paulo the Clown. Of course this only happened after Douglas McPherson, author of Circus Mania, informed me it was World Circus Day when we were away—who could resist the circus?

Month five's 'Do Something I've Never Done Before' challenge turned out to be a wonderful month of opportunities. I made a fairy garden with my daughter, crafting queen Nicola Grice taught me how to make a quilt cushion cover, and I had very girlie eyelash extensions by the gorgeous Ellie. The most amazing challenge that month though was going into my local junior school to run a workshop on Emotional Freedom Techniques (EFT) to help the year six children cope with the stress and anxiety of their SATs.

Month five finished on a very high note when I scared myself to death by going a zip wire. My knees were knocking for days after that challenge.

In month six I motivated an army of readers to declutter, grow their own vegetables and salad and try the odd meat-free dinner.

With six months completed and the next six months stretching ahead I was energised and raring to go. For the remainder of the year I would have to, at various points, cope without television, Facebook, my car, or in the case of month seven, black clothing. I'd have to put on my travel writing head for month eight and report from London, Cornwall, Warwick and York, plus any other pretty towns I might stumble across. My biggest challenge of the year—NaNoWriMo, which is a competition to write a 50,000 word novel in one month—was scheduled for month eleven and then in month twelve I would be turning my hand to homemade gifts.

If you are feeling motivated to achieve something for yourself and are wondering how to achieve it then read on.

Try to look beyond your usual routines. There is a land of amazing possibilities out there, so be daring, be creative, stand out, do things and go to places you've never been before.

Repeat after me—*'This is the best year of my life!'*

Month 7

APPRECIATE WHAT I HAVE BY GIVING SOMETHING UP

"I enjoy a challenge."

AS I prepared for my month seven challenges, the weatherman had promised a spell of sunshine, ice creams and paddling pools.

What a wonderful way to start a challenge and for this month I had to be grateful for what I have by giving something up. Sounded simple enough on paper. I split the month into four and gave something up for a week at a time. This included giving up my car, Facebook and television, but I found week 27 to be the hardest of all.

At the request of my daughter, I had to give up wearing black clothing. You may think that sounds very trivial but I DARE you to go through your wardrobe and remove everything black—see, I'm not the only one who has an ocean of black fabric in their closet, am I!

My daughter is always telling me off when we go clothes shopping as I navigate my way to the dull and boring black outfits. She rolls her eyes and says, 'Mum, get something colourful.'

Of course at twelve years of age she rocks the whole multi-coloured leggings, layered T-shirt look, but I like my comfy clothes and I like them to be black.

So I decided to appease her and agreed to go one week without wearing ANY black item of clothing. I realised the magnitude of this challenge when, on day one, with bleary eyes and bed hair, I fished around in my underwear drawer for any other colour of pants! (Note to self—pants situation critical.)

Fortunately I did find the appropriate undergarment and could move on to the rest of my outfit but yet again I hit a snag—my work uniform was BLACK!

So at 6 a.m. I found myself digging through the very large ironing pile to find an old white tunic and tan coloured trousers which had been my uniform five years ago—oh God, would my backside fit into the trousers? This challenge could get embarrassing.

Panic over, it all fit (snugly) and I could at least continue with my working day. Fast forward to the 3 p.m. school run and thank goodness for blue denim.

With two minutes to spare I stood in my jeans and bra (white one) looking at 25 black tops. If I turned up at school in just my underwear my daughter would disown me, then I remembered a multi-coloured T-shirt I'd bought for an eighties fancy dress party—yes, I wore it.

I didn't think it was possible for an eye roll from a twelve-year-old to stop me in my tracks but hey, this challenge was never going to be easy—on either of us apparently. So, after receiving strict instructions to stay in the car from now on, we made our way home.

I decided that some planning was needed if I was going to last the week stress-free. I took out everything I owned that was black from my wardrobe, drawers and even the shoe rack.

The result was quite surprising; looking at my now colourful rail of clothing, (yes there were a few bright bits and bobs hiding in there) I realised I was 'smiling'. Don't get me wrong, I smile all the time so this isn't a new phenomenon, but it was the reason for my smile that intrigued me. The colours were lifting my mood.

When I teach my meditation classes I include a topic on 'colouring in' and how this simple act can calm the mind and help us be in the now. As part of the topic we also look at our choice of colouring pencil to give us a guide as to what mood we are in—colour therapy.

How amazing that this simple lesson could overlap into my day-to-day life.

Over the course of the week I tried to wear a different colour each day and the results were quite astonishing:

- Red top—I cleaned the house top to bottom and felt very 'active'.

- I had to attend a funeral and so instead of the usual black attire I chose to wear navy. I felt quite peaceful despite the upsetting circumstances.

- When I wore my pink jumper I enjoyed an entire hour of me time, chilling with a book, before spending the evening doing lovely family stuff with my children.

- When I wore my green T-shirt I noticed that nothing seemed to bother me.

So what do the colours actually mean?

- **Red:** Commands action, helps express passion, joy and anger.

- **Blue:** Creates a feeling of serenity and trust, good for communicating your needs.

- **Pink:** Loving colour, promotes a calm atmosphere and relieves tired muscles.

- **Green:** Great for balancing, self-love and stress relief.

Over the week I found myself searching for brighter colours to wear and I loved the way each piece of clothing impacted on my mood—my inner sunshine emerged.

I looked forward to getting my tropical clothes out and carrying on with the colour challenge. Although black can give the illusion of a slimmer body, it can also drain your emotions and leave you feeling gloomy. It's a habit I appear to have taken on since my divorce and coming to this realisation—albeit ten years later—had an astonishing impact on my well-being.

My challenge also sparked a rather hilarious discussion with my meditation class about colour-coordinated underwear—I think that's a whole challenge in itself!

Leaving the car at home for week 28 just happened to coincide with a UK heatwave but I refuse to call this cheating. When I decided to include 'Appreciate What You Have By Giving Something Up' as one of my resolutions, I knew each item would have to be important, otherwise where would the challenge be?

In the grand scheme of things this probably wasn't such a hard challenge as I do very low mileage, but when you have a car you do use it all the time regardless of whether the shop is two or twenty miles away—or is that just me?

What I did learn during my car-free week was to appreciate the convenience of being mobile and the ability to 'pop out' whenever and wherever we want.

I thoroughly enjoyed walking my daughter to and from school—the beautiful weather obviously a factor—but I did find food shopping a bit tricky. As I struggled back from the town centre, my knuckles grazing the floor as I wrestled with four heavy shopping bags, I really did miss my Honda. On the plus side I can now touch my toes without bending my knees.

As I was feeling quite smug about this challenge and enjoying the fresh air and exercise, I started wondering if my small, seven-day stint had had any impact on the environment. So I took to Google to find out the answer and was very surprised at what my research uncovered.

I discovered the Carbon Footprint Calculator, a fabulous site that enables you to see how your life is impacting the environment. Enter your country and the dates you wish to calculate to and from. The site gives you a selection of tabs to choose from which include house, car, flights, motorbike etc; fill in the relevant information and then click the green 'offset' button. This takes you to a link whereby you can donate to a worthy cause to offset your carbon footprint should you wish. The causes include:

- Clean Energy
- Reforestation in Kenya
- UK Tree Planting
- Certified Emission Reduction

By not using my car for one week I saved 0.02 tonnes, not a lot really but then I only travel approximately 60 miles. Over the course of a year this equates to 1.18 tonnes based on my low mileage (not taking into account holiday and weekend travel.) The average footprint in the UK is 9.80 tonnes.

I found this really interesting and ended up working out my entire household's usage with scary results. I would need to plant a lot of trees to offset our lifestyle.

By switching my car for walking shoes I not only saved on petrol but I also managed to help the environment, albeit on a small scale, and it also meant I was exercising and bonding with my daughter as we walked and chatted—priceless.

Week 29 loomed and I realised that when I added a week of 'No Facebook' to my challenge list I honestly didn't think it would be a tough one—it was only for seven days—no problem. How wrong could I have been?

I *really* missed it, which confirmed a niggling suspicion I had about myself—I am a social media fanatic.

Cynics will tell us that all this mumbo jumbo of social media has caused the fall of our society; my own dad can't understand why I comment, like pages and post pictures, and I quote 'for the entire world to see'. I have tried to explain the privacy settings to him but this is the man who couldn't find the 'B' on his keyboard and had to call me.

For me, Facebook allows me to interact with my family in Yorkshire and my friends who are scattered across the globe.

On a business level, I am able to share news and events about my own holistic company with my clients, as well as people who may not be able to utilise my spa facilities but find my ramblings quite interesting.

Facebook is also great fun. As an avid reader, I follow a number of authors on Facebook. I love the opportunity to interact with the 'real' person, they're not just a name on the front cover anymore. You can get involved, join discussions and add your own book reviews; it all makes one feel a part of their community.

As a writer I relish that connection and adore the feedback I receive about my blog, newsletters and stories. I know having that reader-author relationship will help me to create better stories and characters for my own books.

So a week without Facebook—could you cope?

I have friends who log on intermittently, I have friends who last logged on in 2008 and I have friends who, like me, stay logged on and comment every 30 seconds.

In my humble opinion you get out of social media what you are prepared to put in. I love sharing some of the affirmation pages as I know which quote will be just what one friend may need. The funny sayings I share often receive multiple likes or re-shares which means we all have the same warped sense of humour. Anything beer-related gets a great response and anything child-related gets an 'OMG, how much have they grown.' This is normally followed by a direct mail catch up with friends living in Australia.

Facebook, together with the many other social media platforms, makes the world a smaller and more intimate place. Old friends, new friends, colleagues, clients, celebrities, fans and, of course, family are only a click away.

Going without Facebook, however, did give me time to re-evaluate who I connect with. It became apparent quite quickly who I missed interacting with. Take five minutes to evaluate your own Facebook page, cull any acquaintances who don't make you feel good or post statuses like 'big shop done for another week'—actually I think I may have posted that once.

Rekindle friendships and support one another's business ventures and successes, follow interesting pages where you learn something new every day. Comment on photographs, laugh at the funny stuff and embrace the social media age.

My challenge to you is this:

Why not give Facebook up for a week—it will either kill or cure you of your social media habits.

- **KILL:** I miss the news, views and updates and will never be without my Facebook family again. My name is _____ and I am a Facebook addict and proud of it.

- **CURE:** Not a problem, I didn't miss it and with all that extra time I wrote an epic novel and now have a multi-million-pound publishing deal.

On week 30 I was happy to be reunited with my beloved Facebook account, but had to say goodbye to another of my lifelines—the television. Thank goodness for the radio; Heart West Midlands FM kept me up-to-date with all the news coverage and I was also lucky enough to share my challenge with the West Midlands dynamic duo, Ed James and Rachel New, on their *Breakfast Show*, live on air.

Ed and Rachel were running a feature on closures, prompted by a main route in and out of the city being closed for refurbishment. They were asking their listeners to call in with their own 'closures'. As I'm an avid fan of the show I thought I'd give them a ring and see if they could assist me with closing down my telly—of course this simply meant switching it off but I do like to be theatrical. After Ed and Rachel counted me down I very dramatically pulled the plug on the fifth member of our family—my five minutes of fame was over and what a giggle it had been.

As the week came to an end I realised that I hadn't really missed the television. After the 'No Facebook' challenge, I did worry that I may develop a nervous twitch, but the 'No Television' challenge had been fairly easy. The only night I did struggle was Friday.

The children and I have a film night every Friday. We pick a DVD and stock up on popcorn, we close the curtains and pretend we're at the cinema—being a single mum with three kids we can't always afford the real thing and have to improvise.

It was tough when I realised that film night wasn't allowed. Instead of a DVD we played hangman, Pictionary and a board game called 'Are you smarter than a ten year old?'—which apparently, I am not.

You may wonder what I did do without the television to entertain me. In one week I read two and a half books, wrote two short stories and a flash fiction compilation, I did some research for my Young Adult novel and even attempted a lipogram (a poem where you are not allowed to use a specific letter, for example 'C').

This challenge got me wondering how much time I actually waste watching *Friends* repeats so I did a few sums and in one week I'd managed to claim back 17 hours.

Will I be plugging the set back in again? It wouldn't bother me either way—the kids may disagree—although if you told me *The Vampire Diaries* was starting tomorrow I'd fight you for the remote control!

Month Seven = Mission Completed

Month 8
GET OUT AND ABOUT MORE

"I am open to new experiences."

WHEN I decided on my month eight challenge of getting out and about more, it obviously had to coincide with the school holidays. In the past we had taken the obligatory week's break and then squandered the rest of the summer. As a new school year arrived I would kick myself for not doing more and not taking the kids to see more of our fabulous country. I wanted this challenge to change that and so we started week 31 in a beautiful village called Downderry, near Looe on the south coast of England.

I spent my childhood exploring the coves, crabbing and rock pooling along the Cornish coastline but for some reason I'd never been back with my children.

This is partly because my parents own a holiday caravan in Somerset which we are fortunate enough to be able to use, and partly because when I became single again, with sole responsibility for three little lives, it scared me to death to think of driving across the country without another adult for support.

My confidence may have soared in certain areas of my life but it had plummeted in others. A holiday to Cornwall may seem fairly mundane to some, but for me and my family it was a huge landmark, one of which I am very proud.

Safety is a huge concern for any parent but as a single mum it can overwhelm everything you do and sometimes hinder your decisions.

The south coast is always guaranteed to be a hit with families and we were no exception. We do own a tent and we love the outdoor life, but for this trip I wanted to bask in a little luxury and so we hired a small cottage.

I used Cottages 4 You which has a selection of 13,000 cottages to choose from in England, Ireland, Italy and France. Booking is straightforward using their website and just before we left for our trip they e-mailed me a what's on guide and a list of places of interest close to our chosen property—a nice touch. (Links can be found at the end of the book.)

Once we had checked into our stunning sea view cottage, we were free to explore the delights of Cornwall.

So what's on offer to entertain the children? My kids would have been happy on the beach every day and we certainly had the weather for it, but as a happy balance we intermingled our beach time with sightseeing. Our favourite places of interest were:

- **Looe:** In medieval times there were two towns on opposite sides of the River Looe; the east had the fishing harbour and the west was a quiet seaside town. They are now joined by a bridge and together make a picturesque holiday destination. Looe hosts a music festival in September which is worth a visit.

- **Polperro:** A perfect Cornish fishing village and one of my favourite places in England.

- **Plymouth:** A treasure trove of family attractions including one of the world's most famous lighthouses, Smeaton's Tower, built in 1759, museum and art gallery, The National Marine Aquarium, Theatre Royal, ice rink, lido and so much more.

- **Mount Edgcumbe:** Set in the Grade I listed Cornish Gardens, an 865-acre country park on the Rame Peninsula, south-east Cornwall. This stunning park is well worth a visit. We took a packed lunch and walking boots and spent the entire day exploring the grounds, beaches and walks around the estate. The gardens are immaculate and the views across to Plymouth are incredible.

There are so many places to visit in Cornwall and I haven't even scratched the surface. That's half the excitement of holidays—finding your own special place and making memories.

As our tour continue, we moved north, leaving the wondrous Cornish coastline behind for the green fields of Somerset, a county rich in cider and cheese, caves and beaches and, of course, world-famous music festivals.

Somerset has more attractions than days in the year so we were spoilt for choice. In our mad dash up the country I only managed to touch on two of the attractions available but if you are planning a trip to Somerset then log on to www.visitsomerset.co.uk for more wonderful trips to enhance your holiday or fill a day off.

One of my own personal favourite places for a holiday or day trip is Glastonbury. I'm not talking about Wellingtons and festival gear. Glastonbury may be well-known for its festival but for me this is a place of mysteries, myth and legend. King Arthur is believed to have been active here, South Cadbury being a possible site for Camelot.

GLASTONBURY ITSELF is a mecca for anyone interested in holistic living, crystals and New Age. Jeans, T-shirts and fairy wings are the norm!

On a day trip to this magical place you can take in the range of quaint shops, visit the abbey with its impressive grounds (perfect for picnics so plan ahead and pack your chicken wraps and crudités) and finish with a walk up to Glastonbury Tor which has stunning 360 degree views from the summit.

My children love Glastonbury as much as I do and have explored every inch of the abbey and purchased many a crystal from the quaint high street shops, but what if you don't have a family of hippies? Where do you go on your day trip then?

I WOULD suggest you head towards the River Axe and the nearby Wookey Hole Caves. These are Britain's most spectacular caves which have existed for over a million years. Earliest man, hunting with stone weapons, lived in the caves, as did the Celtic people of the Iron Age. It was believed that an evil old woman resided in the caves in the 18th century; she was turned to stone by a monk using holy water. The legend of the Wookey Hole Witch is still strong today and her skull, found in 1912 by archaeologist Herbert Balch, can be seen in the museum.

The caves are incredibly impressive and I marvelled at how anyone could live there as I descended Hell's Ladder to the Witch's Kitchen, surrounded by shining stalagmites which erupted from the rock around me while I dodged the dripping stalactites.

The legends are brought to life by the wonderful guides who, in my opinion, must be able to recite the history of the caves in their sleep.

Once you return to the surface, the fun continues and there are plenty of attractions for kids of all ages. Wookey Hole has a paper mill, pirate island adventure golf, cave museum and cave diving museum. There is a circus show and circus museum (complete with petrified mermaids discovered off the coast of Bali in 1823), a mirror maze and an old penny arcade. There is a dinosaur park and my own personal favourite—Fairy Land. It's a fantastic day out for all the family.

The restaurant serves a fantastic homemade steak pie but there are plenty of picnic benches if you want to take your own lunch.

I love Somerset and return as often as I can. There is so much to keep the kids entertained, but if, like me, you're drawn to the legends and rugged landscapes then pack up the car and go there on your next day off.

Take in the traditional market towns, country houses and parks. Visit the Georgian splendour of Bath, or Wells, the smallest city in England, a medieval jewel at the foot of the Mendip Hills.

Of course for all the book lovers out there, no trip to Somerset is complete without exploring the open moorland of Exmoor National Park and breathing in the air of Lorna Doone's county.

HOLIDAYS ARE a wonderful way to explore foreign lands or distant parts of your own country. Venturing far and wide in search of an escape is a wonderful adventure but in our month eight quest to get out and about, we nearly overlooked the simplest destination of all— our own doorstep.

By this I don't mean open the patio doors and take in the view of your petunias, what I do mean is take in the delights of your local area.

DURING MY MONTH eight challenge I had driven approximately 520 miles (836km), taking in the Cornish coast and the breathtaking beauty of Somerset, but for week 33 I chose to stay closer to home and look at what was available in my local area.

We live eight miles (12km) from Britain's second city, Birmingham. An amazing city full of rich architecture, museums and famed for its food festivals.

We also live 23 miles (37km) from Stratford-upon-Avon, home of William Shakespeare and the Royal Shakespeare Theatre. A 30-minute drive will take me to Warwick, Royal Leamington Spa, Drayton Manor Theme Park and Zoo, or Cadbury World.

During the summer months my own hometown of Solihull hosts numerous events such as a food festival, craft markets, activities for the kids and music events.

Once you begin to take a closer look at what is available on your doorstep you will be pleasantly surprised.

Totally unrelated to my month eight challenge, I attended a writing workshop, hosted by the incredible Stan Nicholls, bestselling author of the *Orcs* series, at a venue just 15 minutes from my house. This was a place I had passed a hundred times, I knew it was there but it never occurred to me to visit with the children.

It was Sarehole Mill, a working watermill built in 1750, but best known for where J.R.R. Tolkien spent part of his childhood. He later used the surroundings as inspiration for *The Hobbit* and *The Lord of the Rings*.

If funds are tight then enjoy a 'staycation' and look closer to home for a day out. I enjoyed planning my 'Get Out And About More' challenge and it became a challenge in itself to find the most interesting places to visit.

HAVING SPENT a week rushing around our local area we then embarked on a cultural visit. Who said a city break had to be for couples looking for a romantic getaway?

Don't get me wrong, as we sat on the train heading to London we were surrounded by doe-eyed lovers, but it certainly didn't deter this single mum and her band of teens.

There are plenty of cities here in the UK for us to choose from for an overnight stay, each one offering its visitors a wealth of historical sights, attractions and hotels.

If you are planning a trip around the UK or visiting us from afar, take a look on Wikipedia for an impressive list of cities; Bath, Birmingham, Cambridge, Leeds, Manchester, Newcastle-upon-Tyne, Nottingham, Sheffield, York, Wells...these are just a few from an extensive list. The directory also covers cities in Scotland, Wales and Northern Ireland.

I HAD taken my children to our capital once before and they loved it so much that that was their city of choice for our month eight challenge.

What I didn't want to do was take them around the main sights we had seen before—as wonderful as Big Ben, Buckingham Palace, Madame Tussauds and Piccadilly Circus may be, there are so many other areas worth visiting.

Always conscious of my budget I chose a Premier Inn for our bed and breakfast needs. Premier Inn County Hall is at the base of the London Eye so this hotel was a perfect base to explore from. It's on the south bank of the Thames and that is where we started our walking tour.

When I've taken a city break with my mum we have invariably ended up in the shops—it's a girl thing. If my children even suspected I was heading in the direction of Oxford Street they would throw me in the Thames, however, there is one particular shop that they know I am physically incapable of walking past—a bookshop. I was, therefore, over the moon when we found Foyles bookshop, but imagine my delight when ten minutes later we stumbled across the Southbank Book Market. Rows and rows of tables crammed with paperbacks in every genre imaginable. My idea of heaven.

When they did finally drag me kicking and screaming from the stacks of paperbacks, we enjoyed a leisurely stroll along the river, taking in the Tate, Shakespeare's Globe Theatre, Sir Francis Drake's ship and finally ended up on the HMS Belfast.

We crossed the river and ate our lunch sitting alongside the Tower of London before heading towards Hyde Park to see the Diana Princess of Wales Memorial Fountain. The park was full of families enjoying the sunshine and having a paddle in the fountain, the atmosphere was buzzing and we couldn't help but get caught up in the fun, with the addition of ice cream of course.

When we had walked along the Thames after dinner the previous evening, to take in the full moon as it hung above the city, I had casually pointed out the 'second star to the right' and realised our trip to Hyde Park would not be complete without seeing Peter Pan's statue.

I adore the vibrancy of London and yet it was lovely to spend time out of the main rush of the city streets, exploring the parks and river bank attractions on this city break. I will definitely look at spending more time in South Bank as this has a treasure trove of boutiques (must take Mum!) bars, restaurants and attractions together with art galleries and historical buildings.

For the final week of my 'Get Out And About More' challenge I was able to sneak away for a couple of nights with just my daughter. I love all my kids and we had had an amazing six weeks but to have some mummy-daughter time was quite precious. I left the destination up to her and thankfully she chose the walled city of York in North Yorkshire (and not Milan or Paris as my budget may not have stretched that far).

A girlie trip is very different to a family holiday when my sons are with us. For a start my daughter didn't moan when we found the shops, in fact she cost me a small fortune in new clothes and I won't even tell you how many books she bought in Waterstones.

For a girls' getaway, York is a fabulous city. Obviously my daughter is slightly too young to hit the clubs and bars so I can't comment on the nightlife, but we did walk our legs off exploring the walls, which have defended the city since Roman times, and discovering the winding, cobbled streets.

No trip to York is complete without taking in the fantastic York Minster, one of the largest cathedrals of its kind in northern Europe. I found an interesting website which reveals the work of archaeological excavations in the Minster and will shed light on York's Dark Ages. Take a look at www.yorkminster.org.

There are plenty of museums to explore in York. If I cast my mind back to my own childhood, any museum trip we took normally consisted of looking at dusty old stuff and being told to be very quiet. At least today most museums cater to children and the York Castle Museum is definitely one of them. Open daily (except on 25th and 26th December and 1st January) this attraction is not to be missed. The youngsters can tour the museum as detectives and find the clues hidden around the exhibit; there are plenty of staff dressed in Victorian costume on hand to help the budding Sherlocks.

The museum has a selection of rooms from different periods of time together with a collection of toys from the 1900s through to modern times. My daughter found it highly amusing to see my Sindy doll in the 'OLD TOY' section—I was not amused!

They have recreated a Victorian street, complete with schoolroom, police cell and cobbled street. Every shop on the street is based on a real York business which was in operation between 1870 and 1901.

Close to the museum is Clifford's Tower, an impressive building which was the keep of York Castle and built between 1245 and 1272. During the school holidays there are plenty of activities going on and the view from the top of the tower is breathtaking.

One of my daughter's favourite shops is to be found on The Shambles, a beautiful cobbled street in the heart of the city. This is York Glass Ltd. She bought herself a lucky black cat, handmade from glass, and she was then handed a challenge of her own—to follow the fabulous York Cat Trail and find the 21 lucky cats that have been placed on buildings in York for around two centuries. The original cats were put up to frighten rats which could carry the plague, but as time passed they became a beacon of good luck and good health.

The walled city of York is a magical place for a girl of any age and both of us thoroughly enjoyed our girls' getaway. I asked my daughter which part of our trip she had loved the most, was it the Victorian street, the amount of history York has amassed in its two millennia of existence or the stunning Jorvik Centre which was built on the site where the well-preserved remains of part of Viking Jorvik (York) were discovered. Apparently all this heritage just couldn't compare with, 'Being with you, Mum.'

Priceless!

Month Eight = Mission Completed

Month 9
LEARN SOMETHING NEW

"I am learning every day."

I LOVE the autumn. Not only because the air is crisp and the leaves turn a beautiful colour, not because I can dig out my big jumpers and hide the excess flesh which has been on show all summer, but because the air is full of new beginnings.

Kids return to, or start school, college or university and the shops are full of gorgeous stationery to accommodate their needs—my idea of heaven.

My challenge for month nine was to 'Learn Something New' and there really was no better month to start this in. I have a bucket list the length of my arm of what I would love to learn: photography, Italian, painting, knitting...the list is endless.

BUT WHAT if you would love to learn a new skill, retrain or advance your education but you work full-time, have nine children, three cats and a ferret to look after? The answer is simple:

Distance Learning

I love learning new things and I have taken a number of correspondence courses over the years. When my children were very small it was so easy to put them to bed and then work on an assignment, all with the aim of gaining a qualification or new skill.

It isn't a new phenomenon either; learning through weekly mailed lessons dates back to 1728 when a shorthand teacher, Caleb Phillips, saw an ad in the Boston Gazette which prompted him to look for students requiring a correspondence course.

When I was at college I learned the Pitman version of shorthand and its founder, Isaac Pitman, also taught his lessons in the UK via correspondence in the 1840s. The University of London was the first to offer distance learning in 1858 and by 2008 there were 44 states in America offering online learning programmes.

So what's so good about distance learning?

- You can work with an accredited school anywhere in the world.

- It offers relief from the high cost of education. You can take a postgraduate course and save a significant amount of money.

- Distance learning expands access to training for businesses or education for the general public.

- If you have a disability and are unable to attend a traditional school then this is the perfect way to obtain a good education.

- There are no restrictions to learning should you live in a rural area. The University of Queensland began correspondence courses in 1911 to reach students living in remote areas.

Learning at home may be a lonely pastime but most correspondence courses use a variety of materials from textbooks to online resources and include forums where students can meet and interact.

The Open University offers undergraduate, postgraduate and research degrees, as well as short courses in a wide variety of subjects.

If a degree course is not for you then take a look at Mumsnet which has a wonderful selection of courses for all the mums out there who want to learn a new skill. They offer online courses in starting your own business, and edible gardening made easy, or mini courses in DIY. (Links can be found at the end of the book.)

I completed a *Writers' News* home study course with one-to-one feedback from an incredible tutor. It was done at my own pace, no pressure and I had backup and advice at the click of a button.

OF COURSE, learning something new doesn't necessarily have to be a planned event. We all make mistakes during our lives, some are tiny and others monumental, but the key to recovering is to learn from the lessons these mistakes provide.

I encountered this first-hand and I held my hands up...'it's a fair cop' as they say. As week 37 began I found myself attending a Speed Awareness course. Not because my jogging career was taking off in a big way but because I was caught by a mobile speed camera doing 34 mph in a 30 mph zone.

My options were—three points on my licence and a £100 ($133 USD) fine, or I could attend a four-hour course and only pay £85 ($113 USD). I opted for the course.

- **Lesson Number One:** Consequences

I am self-employed so I lost half a day's earning. I was not alone... out of the 25 people on the course, 90% had either taken a day's holiday or had lost earnings.

We must have looked a sorry bunch, with glum faces and arms crossed in a 'I don't want to be here' pose, however, four hours later I was astonished at how much I had learned, how wrong I had been and how much fun I'd had.

The course was run by TTC 2000 which is a national driver training organisation, and our hosts for the day, Paul and Chris, were a well-trained double act. They were warm and friendly and didn't point a finger or slap any wrists.

We began with a simple quiz. It was at this point I realised with absolute horror how much I'd forgotten about the Highway Code.

- **Lesson Number Two:** Complacency

As a holistic health practitioner I have to keep up-to-date with my CPD (Continuing Personal Development), so why is driving any different? I was amazed at just how much information I had forgotten since my driving test many years ago.

Here are a few questions for you to try:

1. What is a 'repeater' sign?
2. For a car, what is the national speed limit on a single carriageway?
3. How would you know where a 40 mph, or 50 mph speed limit applies?

Answers on a postcard please!

- **Lesson Number Three:** Speeding is a Waste of Time

During the course we looked at some of our 'excuses' for speeding. The most popular was—being late.

Q. You are late for a meeting or getting the kids to school, so you speed. On a local road you may do 35 mph instead of 30 mph. How much faster would you get to your meeting/school?

A. Can you believe that all that stress and rushing around only gains you 18 seconds?

If you did 80 mph instead of 70 mph on the motorway you would only gain 64 seconds but more shockingly perhaps is that you would have used 25% more fuel.

Lesson Number Four: Changing Bad Habits and Managing Speed

We were given another quiz at this point—to fill in the blanks—take a look and see if you can work out what the letters could stand for.

C O A S T

Any idea?

It's Concentration, Observation, Anticipation, Space and Time.

I was shocked to discover that in the space of 60 minutes' driving time we only concentrate on the act of driving for 15 minutes—where on earth is our brain for the other 45 minutes?

We were taught a really great trick to help with our observation. As you drive around town say aloud what you see around you, for example—car, road sign, cyclist, junction, dog, school. My kids thought I'd gone mad when I started doing this but in the end they joined in and it was quite a fun game. The surprising thing for me was as I was Concentrating and Observing my environment and Anticipating what was ahead, I lifted my foot off the accelerator and slowed down without even thinking about it—try it for yourself, it works.

Lesson Number Five: Recognising Speed Limits

This topic was an eye-opener for many of us and I was amazed at how much I got wrong about speed limits on varying roads. We discussed motorways, rural and urban roads and looked at single and dual carriageways. In fact I began to wonder how I ever managed to pass my test in the first place.

We were given yet another top tip on how to remember the speed limits and I'm going to share this with you. *(NB This course applied to roads in England.)*

Is the road you are on a motorway?

Yes: then it's 70 mph (unless stated otherwise)

If not then follow these rules:

Does it have street lights?

YES: Then it's 30

NO: National Speed Limit applies

If it's a 20, 40, 50, 70, there will be a sign to tell you.

Take a moment to reflect on your own driving. Consider where, when and why you normally speed and how you could change it in the future.

ON MY way home from the course I took my time, shouted out everything I could see and stopped at least a car length from the car in front at the traffic lights. I do believe I even shook my head and gave a little tut when someone sped past me as I happily trundled along at 30 mph, stress-free, enjoying the view and grinning from ear to ear. I don't remember my school detentions ever being so much fun.

Why not keep up-to-date with the Highway Code online? This is an ideal way of relearning and can be very helpful when the time comes for your own children to learn to drive.

If you are anything like me, you will have a long list of things you would like to learn.

As week 38 began I was able to tick one more thing off my list—knitting! Yes, at the sprightly age of 42 I had finally picked up a pair of needles and clickety-clacked away to my heart's content.

Don't ask me *why* I wanted to learn to knit. My grandma was a seamstress and could run up a three-piece suit in next to no time, my mum followed in her footsteps and then expanded her creativity to cake decorating and card making, and I don't remember either of them knitting. Maybe I used to knit in a previous life? Whatever the reason, I had this burning desire to learn and as luck would have it, my very wonderful friend, Sarah White, happened to be the best knitter I knew.

Armed with her bag of wool and a selection of needles, Sarah very patiently began my first lesson. I used short 4mm needles and chose a gorgeous blue wool flecked with red and pink. Sarah cast on for me as she wanted me to get a feel for the stitch before teaching me anything as complicated as casting on or off.

Starting slowly I manoeuvred the needle up the back of the stitch, wound the wool around and looped it back through, Sarah watched as I carefully started another stitch. She was full of praise as I managed to complete my first row—I was exhausted.

I had watched Sarah knit many times before and she goes so fast my eyes begin to blur after a while; she knits and she natters and she watches the telly, pets the cat and instructs the household on what jobs need doing and never drops a stitch. I watch in awe as she creates beautiful jumpers and cardigans.

Once I got the hang of it Sarah let me knit a few rows as she made a cuppa. I was concentrating so hard I gave myself a headache. This wasn't turning out to be the relaxing pastime I thought it would be.

Roll of the shoulders, crack of the neck, sip of the hot tea and back to it—like on a production line.

After several rows my knitting 'yoda' inspected my work...I had somehow managed to add a few extra stitches and my work of art was veering off at an angle. Sarah expertly got me back on track and away I went again.

It took me some time to knit a handful of rows but the more I did, the more I began to enjoy myself. As one of my favourite Pinterest quotes says 'Allow yourself to be a beginner, no-one starts at the top.'

With my first lesson completed, Sarah left me with the needles and the ball of wool so I could keep practising. As it so happened I fell ill a few days later and took great comfort in sitting up in bed with my knitting.

TAKING PART in this resolution challenge had opened up so many opportunities for me and I was able to do so many of the things I had only ever dreamed of.

Quite a few people have told me some of the things they wish they had done or learned. All I would say is do it today—do it now! Don't keep putting it off. If you fancy learning to knit, then have a go, if you want to crochet—do it. Learn something new and I guarantee you will feel a million dollars and reduce all that stress and tension that plagues daily life.

Working as a holistic health practitioner means I am privileged to be a part of someone's life journey—that could be a road to better health, much needed relaxation or an understanding ear and support.

I am very vocal about my own life and don't hide the highs and lows I have experienced; in fact I use these experiences to help me be a better practitioner. I left a physically and emotionally abusive marriage, taking my three children under the age of five with me. To say I had hit rock bottom would be an understatement, but I dragged myself kicking and screaming back to reality.

As I recovered and tried to find myself, I learned how to laugh and smile again, I learned from others how to interact, trust and love again. It's incredible how much we do learn from those people that surround us on a daily basis.

To complete my month of learning something new, I thought it would be fun to include all the things I'd learned during my own journey and reaffirm my lessons.

So here are my top 15 tips:

1. **Laugh:** Children laugh around 300 times a day. Children's laughter is one of the most amazing sounds in the world. How many times do you think the average 40-year-old laughs? It's four! Take a leaf out of the kids' book and have a giggle.

2. **Drink More Water:** My clients know that at some stage in their appointment I will tell them to drink more water—it's a standing joke now. The main excuse is that they forget, which is fair enough as I used to do exactly the same. I now leave a glass by my kettle so every time I make a cuppa, the glass is there to remind me to drink a glass or two while the kettle boils. Visual reminders are great.

3. **Be Optimistic:** I have always been a glass is half-full kind of person and I believe this has got me through some horrific moments. Optimists also tend to be luckier in life as having a positive outlook attracts positive things your way.

4. **Declutter:** Regularly. I know that when my energy is low, the cupboard under the stairs needs clearing out. It's classic feng shui, having a good clear-out makes room for new opportunities and experiences (and people) to enter your life. Start small, if you haven't worn a particular outfit for over a year—donate it to charity.

5. **Let Your Kids Argue:** Sibling rivalry is an important part of growing up (as my brother will confirm). I always

intervened when my three children started shouting at each other. I would break it up and separate them and huff about the house for half an hour, but after reading an article in *Psychologies Magazine* about siblings and how they interact, I stopped getting involved. The first time I didn't mediate I hid in the kitchen and just listened. The arguing started, they shouted and slammed the doors but I still stayed out of it. I was stunned when just five minutes later they were all happy again and playing their game together. I've stayed out of it ever since and my house is much calmer for it.

6. **Meditate:** When people visit my house they tend to stay for ages, not because my conversation is especially scintillating, nor because I bake the most amazing cream puffs, (I don't!) it's because my home is a sanctuary of calm and peace. I run meditation classes from home, I have crystals in every nook and cranny and I meditate whenever I get five minutes—I think all this calm has seeped into the walls. Calm mind, calm body, calm environment.

7. **Emergency Chocolate:** ALWAYS have emergency chocolate in the house!

8. **Accept Help:** People genuinely want to help. If you found out your best friend was struggling with something, you wouldn't think twice before offering to help them out. So why do we struggle to admit that we may need a guiding hand or a shoulder to cry on? Help is out there, all you have to do is ask.

9. **Believe in Yourself:** Success and failure exist in your mind. It's YOUR choice whether you succeed or fail. YOU are awesome and capable of greatness. Believe

that anything is possible, dream big, make plans and do something to make them a reality. One of my favourite quotes is, 'Act as if it were impossible to fail' by James K. Van Fleet.

10. **Think Before You Speak:** Having been on the receiving end of verbal and emotional abuse I am well aware of the consequences and power of words. What you say to another person can inspire or destroy them—choose what you say very carefully.

11. **Family Time:** Children grow up fast! Enjoying their company as they grow and teaching them morals, manners and the values of family life is an important role for every parent; having fun and being silly is also just as important. When I worked in sales I had a photograph on my desk of me and my children—this visual reminder made me pack up my stuff and leave on time every day.

12. **Look After Your Body:** Think about what you eat and drink. You only get one body so look after it as well as you would your brand new car—lovingly wash it, fill the tank with fuel, maintain the engine with regular MOTs and servicing. As a reflexologist I see people's state of health mapped out on the soles of their feet. It's amazing how many people suffer with digestive issues and are dehydrated. Eat fresh food, fruit and vegetables, drink plenty of water, exercise and moisturise! You can't look after your family if you are broken yourself.

13. **Read More, Clean Less:** This one is fairly self-explanatory!

14. **Be Selfish:** It took me years to get this right. My children always came first as did my ex-husband, I was so-and-so's mum, so-and-so's wife—I didn't exist. When

I found myself alone with three very young children I became totally centred on their wellbeing, their schooling, their happiness and forgot that I was a person too, someone who needed just as much care and attention. So now I realise the value of looking after my own needs alongside those of the children. They value this more, there is more give and take in our relationships and it's taught them to go for what they want too and not be submissive.

15. **I could keep going:** I have hundreds of ideas and affirmations tucked away in my brain but I'm handing over to you for Top Tip #15…what's your favourite lesson? Jot it down on a Post-it note and put it somewhere you will see it daily, to remind yourself just how much you have learned already. Then go out and learn something else.

Month Nine = Mission Completed

Month 10
BE HAPPY AND GRATEFUL

"I am grateful for everything in my life."

MONTH TEN'S challenge was to 'Be Happy and Grateful'. A seemingly easy challenge—or was it? Can you be happy if you've just been made redundant or have been involved in an accident? Can you be grateful if your outgoings are more than your incomings and you struggle to pay your bills?

Negative thoughts take over our waking moments and this can make us forget all the good things in our lives.

When I was a small child I remember sitting down for dinner each evening and saying, 'For what I am about to receive may I be eternally grateful.' I never understood what I was saying until I was older and began to appreciate that my dinner didn't just materialise out of thin air and that there were hundreds of people to thank for getting that pie and chips in front of me.

Take a moment to think of what you are most grateful for; they don't have to be momentous achievements.

Here are my top ten:

1. My gorgeous children who light up my world.
2. Amazing parents who support me in everything I do.
3. A warm, cosy bed.

4. My good health.

5. A beautiful home.

6. Friends whom I love dearly.

7. My books.

8. An abundance of inspirational clients who keep my business flowing.

9. Being single and having total control over the television remote.

10. Social media (I know, I know, I can't help it—it's addictive!).

We eat dinner together as a family every night. As we tuck into whatever concoction I have whipped up, my son begins his usual routine—'best and worst thing of the day'.

We take it in turns to say the best thing that has happened and the worst thing. Here are a few examples:

- **Best:** I got ten out of ten in my spelling test (that was one of the kids in case you were wondering).

- **Worst:** It's raining and we couldn't play outside at break time.

- **Best:** I found a fiver in an old coat pocket.

- **Worst:** I owed the window cleaner a tenner.

- **Best:** I got a B on my exam paper.

You get the idea. Try it for yourself; it really makes you think about your day and also gives you an opportunity to talk through the 'worst' parts as a family and turn them into positives.

I often advise my clients to keep a journal. This can be for any number of reasons. Writing down thoughts and emotions helps us to deal with a multitude of issues and ailments. Keeping a gratitude journal can be just as powerful.

Every night jot down five to ten things that you are thankful for. Some of the things you write down may be repeated such as—'my car', 'an understanding boss' or 'my children'. Some may be as simple as—'the sunshine', 'crisp autumn leaves', or 'the incredibly dreamy, Ian Somerhalder'.

Doing this on a regular basis reduces stress and anxiety, uplifts you and makes you feel happier as you are stopping those negative thoughts and replacing them with positive ones.

Another saying from my childhood was 'count your blessings'. This is something I do on a daily basis. In a dim and distant part of my life, I didn't think I would survive to see my next birthday and now here I am, a happy, healthy single mum running my own business, writing books and blogging like a pro. I'm so grateful for that.

WHEN I first started writing my blog it was featured in our local paper. The reporter asked me which challenge I thought would be the toughest—interesting question. At the time I said, to be grateful and happy.

In times of stress and worry, happiness can often be the first emotion we switch off and I see this all too often with my clients. You may ask yourself, 'How can I be happy when I've got too many bills to pay?' You may wonder how it's possible to smile when you truly feel that there isn't anything left to smile about.

I began to think about *why* we think we can't be happy and I realised that instead of adding things to our lives in a bid to find this elusive happiness, we actually need to give a few things up:

- **Give up making excuses:** I can't be happy because... STOP! Tell yourself 'Yes, I can be happy and actually I DESERVE to be.'

- **The need to be in control:** Let that go and accept help if and when it's needed; people really do want to help you.

- **Self-defeating chatter:** We all have that inner voice telling us we are stupid, fat or too old to do something. Try listening to that voice and then saying, 'Thank you for your concerns, I appreciate you are there to help but I am in a safe place and happy to continue doing...'

- **Negative friends:** Vampires are REAL! I'm not talking about your sparkling, big hair types, but those friends that suck every ounce of your good energy and pour their own negativity down your throat.

- **Complaining:** Obviously, if you find a severed finger in your soup please do feel free to mention it to your maître d', but otherwise, stop moaning—thoughts become things, so only allow the positive, feel-good vibes to get through.

- **The need to impress other people:** My dad has a notebook full of inspirational quotes he has collected over many years in business. Throughout my life he has fired so many of them at me I feel like a walking inspirational billboard, however, the one that stuck with me was what Eleanor Roosevelt said, 'Only with your consent can someone make you feel inferior.' We can feel an overwhelming need to make people like us and then feel awful when they shoot us down – why? Try to think differently, say to yourself 'I am who I am, take me or leave me.'

- **Unhealthy attachments:** In the same way our negative friends can suck our good emotions from us, we can also latch on to something (or someone) bad for us which has the same detrimental effect. Yes, I am also talking about chocolate!

- **Regrets:** Never look back, always look forward. Don't regret something you did, just learn from it. We all did crazy things when we were in our teens and although you may really wish you hadn't had that tattoo on your bottom, it's a lesson you can pass on to your own children.

- **Living in the past:** Did you know that you concentrate approximately 70% of your energy thinking about your past, 10% pondering your future and the remaining 20% being in the now? You can't change what's already happened, so why worry? Shift your thinking to live in the moment and concentrate on what you can achieve right now, today.

- **Waiting:** Be honest, how many of you have said, 'I'll be happy when…I meet someone/get that job/move house/ publish my book'? STOP. Don't put your life on hold waiting to be happy—BE happy and then the wonderful things you're waiting for will come rushing to your side because you are sending out those happy vibes.

Try and work through the list and see what changes you can make or what you can give up. After all, don't we all deserve to be blissfully happy?

As week 41 arrived I began a challenge that has the ability to make people squirm—compliments. Paying someone a compliment is such a natural thing to do, and you have the ability to make somebody's day. Why then do we squirm when we are on the receiving end of a compliment?

Picture the scene—you have just bumped into an old friend whom you haven't seen for a few months and they've lost four stone in weight. It is an automatic reaction to say, 'Oh Doris, you look amazing!' Your initial reaction is to pay them a compliment because you are genuinely happy for them and they DO look amazing.

Now let's look at the flip side—you are wearing a new coat that took five months to save for and you bump into a friend, they say, 'Oh Doris, I love your coat!'

You say, 'What, this old thing? Oh I've had it in the closet for months!'

Huh?

As children we are taught to be confident, to push ourselves in school and at leisure activities. I tell my own children to act like leaders not sheep, but underlying all this positive self-promotion we are taught by peers that being confident is not always a good thing.

You may be bullied for being smart, pretty or good at sport. In the case of a woman, you may be branded as a flirt, a slapper or worse, if you can engage comfortably with male colleagues.

There is a fine line between confidence and arrogance. We are often conditioned to believe that having all this confidence will turn people off us, leaving us alone and unloved and so we shy away from believing in ourselves.

As we reach adulthood these beliefs are often so ingrained we are unable to shake them off, but this can cause us to become needy, a wallflower in our own life and can often mean we are overlooked when the promotions are handed out.

When we receive a genuine compliment it goes against every nerve in our body to accept it, all thanks to this conditioned upbringing.

So what can we do?

- **Unlearn everything:** Project a secure image of yourself to the outside world. In 2006 I went on a Solo's holiday, my first encounter as a newly divorced woman. The children stayed at home with my parents and I packed my case and flew to Italy. I missed the rep at the front desk and received a note under my door to say she would see me in the hotel bar. This meant I had to go looking for someone I had never met, in a public place where everyone spoke Italian but me! I threw my shoulders back, held my head high and walked as boldly as my wobbly legs would let me, straight up to the barman and asked if he knew the rep. Long story short, she had seen me walk in but assumed I couldn't be the person she was meeting as I looked so confident! I was screaming inside but I'd projected the right image.

- **Pay yourself a compliment:** Why can't you look in the mirror and say 'Hey good-looking'? It worked for Arthur Fonzarelli.

- The toughest one of all is forcing yourself to accept that compliment. This will take practice but it does work. The next time someone pays you a compliment, take a deep breath and say 'Thank you.' Don't dither about thinking of something to say back to them, just accept their praise and smile.

Everyone deserves to be complimented so the next time you are out and about try making somebody's day with a kind word.

If you can't find anyone to compliment then I can point you in the direction of a whole group of people whose very existence relies on receiving compliments…authors.

Writers of fiction, non-fiction and poetry crave and relish a kind word or two. In fact, if you can squeeze a few more words into your compliment then why not leave a review on an author's Amazon page or on Goodreads, Twitter or Facebook. Trust me, they WILL thank you for it.

As I approached the end of month ten I was feeling very grateful, happy, confident and complimentary. This challenge hadn't been as difficult as I had anticipated. To finish off the month I therefore thought it only right to look at how to be silly.

Yes, you read it correctly, I said—'silly'. Why should the kids have all the fun? Autumn has so many opportunities to be silly and my children have had years to get used to how daft I can be at times.

Let's take Halloween, for example; for me this is a magical time and I thoroughly enjoy getting into the spirit (no pun intended) of it. My house is decorated with cobwebs, giant spiders and skeletons and I am suitably dressed up as a witch to greet any little gremlins who call at my door.

Halloween is the perfect time to let your hair down and embrace your inner child. There is so much fun to be had:

- Dressing up as Frankenstein, a ghost, witch or Dracula
- Bobbing for apples
- Carving pumpkins
- Lots of sweets...say no more!

We spend so much time being serious and behaving ourselves in our daily lives that having a moment of silliness can boost your happy hormones and leave you feeling lighter and brighter.

Children are a constant source of amusement, from the silly things they say to the silly things they do, but they are only embracing life and making a host of happy memories.

Do you remember hanging upside down from a tree branch? How about pulling funny faces from the back seat of the car as your parents drove you to school? Did you ever make rock animals with stick-on eyes and pipe cleaners for arms and legs, or open your own zoo?

Everyone needs to embrace their inner child more often and learn to let go of grown-up hang-ups. Try wrapping yourself in toilet paper and taking to the streets on Halloween as a zombie mummy, you may just enjoy yourself.

Month Ten = Mission Completed

Month 11
CONQUER MY FEARS

"I am fearless."

MONTH ELEVEN, the month I had looked forward to and worried about in equal parts since I had added this challenge to my list of resolutions. I was about to become a participant of one of the biggest challenges a writer can face—NaNoWriMo, which stands for National Novel Writing Month.

The competition, now in its 15th year, attracts participants from across the globe. On average, 350,000 writers sign up every year, all dedicated to producing a 50,000 word manuscript in just 30 days.

For the past four years I had wanted to take part in NaNo, but every year I changed my mind at the last minute and ran for the hills. I knew all about 'feeling the fear and doing it anyway' but still I ran. When I started my Resolution Challenge blog I publicly added NaNo to my list of resolutions. This meant I had to take part and therefore couldn't back out; the world knew I was going to do it.

Some people take offence at this competition, saying it doesn't produce anything of quality, but I didn't see it that way. As an A1 procrastinator I had allowed plenty of my own fantasy novel ideas to whirl around the space between my ears. I'd jotted down notes, I even had a Pinterest board dedicated to my characters, but that was as far as I had ever got. Enter NaNo and suddenly I had a plot, an outline and the resources to bring the story to life.

Grammar and spelling might very well be questionable by the end of the month but it didn't matter, I was writing, I was crafting that first draft which, fingers crossed, would be 50,000 words better off by week 48.

You may not be interested in such a challenge but there are plenty of other ways to conquer your own fears in a similar way to NaNo. You could write a diary entry every day for thirty days saying what you are grateful for.

You could try and pay someone a compliment every day for a month, or you could smile at someone new every day and make them feel happy.

I MENTIONED conquering your fears. It is very often our own inner dialogue that causes those fears to manifest and become out of control. It was always my dream to take part in NaNo, but as the month drew closer, I allowed that minx of an inner demon to tell me I couldn't possibly do that—'Pah, who are you kidding? Write 50,000 words? Not a chance!' So as month eleven began, I looked that evil minx straight in the eye and said, 'Back off sister, you can't achieve if you never take part.'

Once I had signed up and began writing, I very quickly came to the conclusion that I was either uber-organised or had absolutely no life whatsoever—I was leaning towards the latter.

Having never taken part in anything so challenging, I knew I would have to use my time wisely. I logged on to the NaNo website and read up on the rules and previous winners' stories, became involved in the forums, and, as recommended, I used the start of the year to plan. I had plotted, built character profiles and I had drawn little maps of what my 'other worlds' would look like—yes, I was *that* neurotic. Of course this all paid off and I made a flying start.

By day six, I had logged 36,523 words. However, as I sat grinning from ear to ear, thinking I was doing really well, I found another

NaNoer who had logged 100,001 and another who reached 51,036 by day three. These guys were the Yodas of the NaNo challenge.

I learned a valuable lesson from these participants: anything is possible if you just get on and do it.

So as a virgin NaNoer, what other lessons did I learn on this crazy quest?

- You are not alone! There were 286,869 writers taking part. Granted, I didn't manage to say hello to *all* of them, but I did make some wonderful new friends from all over the world.

- I can do anything I set my mind to.

- I can enjoy writing to a deadline: In fact it had been a fantastic way to keep me focused. I even had writing time outlined in red pen in my diary.

- It is possible to ask the question, 'If I stab someone in the heart with a magic sword will they die instantly?' and not get arrested. I LOVE forums.

According to the gurus at NaNo HQ, the second week of the competition is notorious for writers abandoning the challenge, but I had no intention of leaving my characters and running for the hills. I was having so much fun developing my fantasy world and seeing what my characters would do next.

With my children watching over my shoulder and providing an audible countdown, I hit 50,296 nine days into the competition. It was the most incredible feeling and having my kids jumping around singing, 'Mum, you did it!' was the icing on the cake.

My characters had become part of the family and although I was ecstatic to have accomplished the challenge, I was a little bit sad when I typed that last word.

Fortunately this challenge had opened up a plethora of ideas and my NaNo draft became book one of a trilogy.

Before I could move on to the next book however, I needed to recap my 50k words and begin the editing process. That was when all my fears began to resurface.

The story had consumed me as I began typing on the first of the month. I was a woman possessed—up at the crack of dawn, typing into the night until I started seeing spots instead of words. I'd get some sleep then start all over again.

My characters had taken on voices of their own and had me chuckling and gasping as new twists uncovered themselves. I'd never enjoyed writing something so much, but as I printed off the 114 crisp sheets of paper I was petrified to see the finished result.

What if it was a pile of rubbish? What if all that humour and tension didn't make it onto the page? What if...? What if...?

Then I remembered the feelings of doubt that had kept me from signing up for NaNo over the years. It was that nagging voice I heard all too often—my own inner critic.

Writing my blog had forced my hand and I had publicly signed up for NaNo, admitting to the world that I was afraid but was going to give it a go anyway—it had been a liberating feeling.

When our inner critic gets going, it becomes all too easy to avoid whatever task we are afraid of; this helps reduce our anxiety, but avoidance is just another word for procrastination.

If I had learned anything from my year as a blogger, it was that my inner critic is just one part of me but it's not all of me. I refused to let it hold me back.

Fighting your inner critic is not easy, in fact, it's best if you don't, as this can just amplify your anxiety. I found the following tips valuable:

- Where has the internal criticism come from? Is it a childhood fear, peer pressure? If you can discover the *where* then you can work on understanding *how* to help yourself.

- Remember that your inner critic is only trying to keep you safe, even when it's complaining. Thank it for caring but ask yourself—is it helping or hurting you?

I realised that the feeling I had deep in my gut, when self-doubt was bubbling under the surface, told me that I was about to embark on something that would change me in some way—it was up to me to work out if that change was for the better.

So, editing a piece of work that I took so much pleasure in writing couldn't be that scary, could it?

As week 48 arrived, the UK was in the comedic clutches of 'I'm a Celebrity...Get Me Out Of Here!' Launched in 2002, the reality show makes for cringeworthy yet compelling viewing.

FOR THOSE of you who don't know, (where have you been?) our national treasures, Ant and Dec, send 12 celebrities deep into the Australian jungle, set them a series of hideous challenges and allow us, the viewers, to vote on their fate—simples.

We can send supermodels over a hundred feet ravine on a tightrope, or make a sports hero eat kangaroo testicles—who wouldn't want to watch that?

Although I had completed my 50,000 word challenge, I continued to join in with the NaNo forums and as I watched 'I'm a Celebrity', I began to look at the similarities between the popular reality show and NaNo.

I'm A Celebrity, Get Me Out Of Here

Sleep Deprivation:

Camping in the jungle surrounded by spiders, wild animals and inclement weather.

Hunger:

If they fail the challenges then the celebs live on rice and beans.

Challenges:

Buried up to your neck in a cockroach pit, eating a crocodile penis, suspended mid-air in a box full of spiders.

NaNoWriMo

Sleep Deprivation:

Can't remember the last time you slept in your bed and not at laptop/kitchen table.

Hunger:

Can't break off...so close to the end of your word count... the fridge is so far away.

Challenges:

Your main character is buried up to his neck in a cockroach pit, your evil mastermind makes his victims eat crocodile penis and your plot twist involves your heroine being suspended in mid-air in a box full of spiders.

It was hard to believe that month eleven was over and I had accomplished one of my biggest dreams. On the first day of the month I had sat at my laptop, opened up a fresh document and set about writing a young adult fantasy story. Nine days later I hit

50,296 words and celebrated with a pepperoni pizza. I threw myself at this challenge with everything I had in me: I blocked out chunks of time in my diary, freed up my weekends and showed the kids how to work the white blob (microwave) and the silver blob (dishwasher). I attached one of my favourite quotes from Barbara Sher, above my desk:

'As soon as you start to pursue a dream, your life wakes up and everything has meaning.'

That's what this challenge was like for me and it paid off—I was a NaNo winner.

I did put down my speedy win to being an over-excited newbie in the land of NaNo. I'm sure that next year I will relax slightly (we can live in hope). Of course I also realise I just publicly signed up for another NaNoWriMo!

ONCE MY word count had been met I didn't sit back and leisurely post on numerous forums for the remainder of the month, oh no. I had started something wonderful and I didn't want to stop, so I carried on writing. I wrote some short stories, started on book two in my Wellbeing Workshop series and plotted out my blog posts for the year to come.

I then received a very positive rejection letter through the post about one of my short stories. It was a 'not now' rather than a 'no' which told me I was on the right track but my timing was wrong on this occasion. How very uplifting.

I was almost as pleased with this outcome as I had been with my NaNo win. I was being taken seriously as a writer, and an editor had taken the time to offer me feedback; pass me another winner badge, I was on a roll!

Many NaNoers did not hit the 50k for numerous reasons and my positive rejection letter got me thinking about how I would have felt if I hadn't managed it.

WOULD I have felt like a failure? Would I have hidden myself away from all the masses of people I had told about my challenge? Hell no! I would have said, 'I gave it a go but it was a "not now" moment. There's always next year'.

If I have learned anything from the challenges I set myself this year, it's that 'failure' is a vital part of my growth. I'm not going to be afraid of the word 'failure' anymore. I choose to call any blip in my life a 'not now' moment.

Everyone faces their own challenges, not necessarily a NaNo writing challenge, but more likely a weight loss challenge, a career change or ill health. Each challenge we face will be so much easier if we know, without any doubt in our minds, that those 'not now' moments may stall us, trip us up or affect other parts of our lives, but if we remember to pursue our dreams, maintain our weight loss campaign, or work on improving our health, then life will wake up for us and we will be back on track in no time.

As if to prove my point, I was honoured to have my interview with the Female Entrepreneur Association appear on their website. It detailed how I had turned my life around after my abusive marriage and started my own holistic health business. There really is no such thing as 'failure' only 'not nows'. (Links to the interview can be found at the back of the book.)

Month Eleven = Mission Completed

Month 12
MAKE HOMEMADE GIFTS

"I am abundant and creative."

MY MUM and I regularly attend our local Hobbycrafts show at Birmingham's National Exhibition Centre. Mum stocks up on her 'crafty' bits and bobs and I carry the bags. It has become a mother-daughter tradition and regardless of the aching muscles and swollen feet, it's a tradition we both enjoy.

The demonstrators on the stands are quite amazing, they can whip up a stunning card in minutes using embellishments, glitter glue and a partridge in a pear tree. They make it look so easy.

My mum is of the same breed. I remember as a child watching her make amazing cakes for customers' birthdays and weddings, homemade jams and marzipan fruits. She then discovered crafting and never looked back, abandoning the oven for Gelli plates and distress inks.

So, as my final challenge of the year was all about making my own homemade cards and gifts, I decided to see if mum's creative gene was hereditary.

One of my favourite stands at the show is Lavinia Stamps'. As an avid fantasy enthusiast I had always been drawn to the displays of twinkling fairies, full moons, playful elves and mystical doorways—in fact, if Tracey Dutton, designer and producer of the stamps, ever developed a wallpaper range I'd be first in line.

The Lavinia Stamps' website is packed with inspiration, sample videos, galleries and projects. You can also watch Tracey on YouTube and really get your creative juices flowing.

It was as I attempted to recreate some of the stunning cards from the website that I realised Mum's creativity gene had skipped a generation. My little cards may well be hidden at the back of the window ledge but I had a lot of fun getting messy with inks, stamps and glue.

Making your own cards and gifts for friends, family, or even teachers and neighbours can be incredibly therapeutic—and thrifty.

As week 50 arrived I decided to make sweet gifts for my friend's housewarming party, crystal packs for my clients and 'friendship bags' for my children.

As a holistic therapist and general lover of all things spiritual, I have an abundance of crystals in my house. I also have a number of ornaments, pictures and oracle cards depicting my own Native American spirit guides, my Chinese zodiac sign and lucky totems related to my life number.

My children are fascinated by spirituality and so I decided to make them a special bag, specific to them, which included all of the above.

It is such an easy thing to create. You will need:

- A small gauze bag or small paper gift bag or tissue paper.
- A crystal relevant to their star sign.
- A picture, photo or totem of their relevant Chinese sign—take a look at Travel China's site:

  www.travelchinaguide.com/intro/social_customs/zodiac/

- I typed up a miniature scroll with their life number details using numerology information

  www.numerology.com

This is what my daughter's gift bag contained:

She is a Cancerian so I put a moonstone crystal in a white gauze bag (white is a good colour for Cancerians—check out Michele Knight's site for more lucky colours www.micheleknight.com). I added a horse key ring as this is her Chinese sign. Her life number is five so I added five of her favourite sweets and a sprinkling of fairy confetti, and I finished it all off with a picture of a woodpecker which is her Native American spirit guide. I knew she would love this gift and I had thoroughly enjoyed making it for her.

HAVE A go at making a personal gift bag for your own children or for friends. It shows that you have put thought and love into each present. It's your choice what you put in. Not a spiritual person? Then why not add in retro sweets, a pair of earrings or miniature nail varnish and a nail file. Got a writer or a book lover in the family? Then add in a novelty pen/pencil set and a quirky notebook...the options are endless.

If the idea of a gift bag doesn't appeal, then do not fear, making your own sweet treats can be just as rewarding.

I had a go at making peppermint creams. They are so easy to make and can be dipped in chocolate for added luxury. Wrapped in tissue and boxed up they make a lovely homemade gift.

You will need:

340g (12oz) icing sugar

1 egg white

A couple of drops of peppermint extract

Food colouring (optional)

- Line a tray with greaseproof paper
- Whisk the egg white until it goes frothy but doesn't go stiff.

- Sift the icing sugar into a bowl and stir in the egg using a wooden spoon until the mixture is stiff
- Knead in the peppermint extract and food colouring (if using)
- Roll out the mixture and using mini cutters, cut out the mints—I used flower and bell-shaped cutters
- Flatten with a fork and place in the fridge for 24 hours

Making your own gifts brings a great sense of achievement and pride so why not have a go? You may end up with an award-winning business idea—remember me when you're famous!

Moving on from my one culinary success, I decided to embrace the savoury palate and have a go at making chutney. My dad loves chutney and as I am hosting the big 'turkey dinner' this year I thought it would be a nice touch to make him a jar of spiced apple chutney.

I decided to utilise the Internet to find a good recipe and during my search I stumbled across the history of chutney. Until that moment I hadn't ever given the origin much thought, but it made for an interesting read, so I thought I would share my findings with you before we all rush off to soak our apples.

Legend has it that a British Army officer by the name of Major Grey, who lived in Colonial India in the 19th century, loved curries so much he made his own chutney using mango, raisins, vinegar, lime, onion, tamarind and spices. This is where some believe the classic mango chutney originates from.

Of course, prior to Major Grey, chutney was a regular guest at any dinner table in India and the exotic spices were brought back to Europe by traders in the 18th century. Usually made as a relish of fresh fruit and spices, chutney is also produced using almost any combination of vegetables, fruits, herbs and spices. There are plenty of varieties out there.

If you are looking for a perfect chutney recipe then you can't go wrong with a good old Delia Smith variety, however, Delia does recommend potting and sealing your chutney for three months before eating—as patience is not one of my strongest traits I opted for an alternative.

I found a recipe for a no-cook spiced apple' variety which only needs to rest for two to three days.

<u>You will need:</u>

2 large apples, peeled, cored and diced

1 red onion, chopped

125g sultanas

80ml red wine vinegar

40g dark brown soft sugar

1/2 tsp ground ginger

1/4 tsp cumin

Pinch cayenne pepper

Seasoning

- Mix all the ingredients together, give them a good stir and season well.
- Pour into a sterilised jar and leave in the fridge for two to three days.
- Shake once a day.
- Shake before eating.
- Keep for up to a week once open.
- Enjoy with cheese and crackers.

Before I had even managed to finish off my chutney I realised that month twelve was at an end. My diary said it, my weekly posts confirmed it and my calendar clearly stated that it was week 52—and what an incredible feeling it was to reach that landmark.

Month Twelve = Mission Completed

THAT'S ALL FOLKS...

FIFTY-TWO WEEKS ago I sat at my parents' house, toasting the end of one year and the start of another wondering how I had let another year roll by without accomplishing anything.

It was that feeling of disappointment that spurred me on to do something about it. Don't get me wrong, I have overhauled my life several times and could write a stack of books on each life-changing event, however this time it was different. I wasn't getting married or having children, I hadn't lost anyone close to me and I certainly wasn't rebuilding my life following a ten year stretch of abuse at the hands of a bully—no, I'd already done that.

I had a successful business doing a job I absolutely loved, working for myself, choosing my own hours to fit around my family, and I was fortunate enough to have a welcoming home, happy and healthy kids and support from my family and friends.

My life was just how I wanted it, but under the surface I still had dreams and aspirations. Goals that I set myself year after year but never actually saw through to the end—writing my book/s, going to night school to learn a new skill, learning a language, being more artistic, reading more...my list was never-ending.

So as I toasted the New Year with my children and parents I made the decision that that year was going to be different—I *was* going to accomplish my resolutions, but how?

The answer to that was so simple. I had always tried to accomplish everything pretty much overnight, which of course was far too overwhelming—even for an avid list maker like myself.

By breaking down the year into bite-sized chunks I could see a more achievable resolution list—twelve months = twelve challenges.

Choosing my challenges was a bit harder. I spent a few hours daydreaming about what I had wanted to achieve over the years. Weight loss, more time to read, enjoy more family time and do more exercise—they all sprang to mind immediately, as did 'stop procrastinating and write your damn book!'

Slowly my list began to take shape. It was then I realised that if I truly wanted to succeed I would have to step outside of my comfort zone and commit to this challenge. The only way I could think to do this was to start a blog and record everything that happened on a public forum.

I had never written a blog in my life so on that first day I signed up to Blogger, and following the simple wizard, I set up what would be my online home for the next twelve months.

Little did I know that that first post, 52 weeks ago would be the start of something amazing. Or that I would have shared my resolutions, the highs and lows of my year, with over 15,000 readers across the globe. I had to learn along the way—I read other people's blogs and got involved in their discussions. They each taught me valuable lessons on how to keep going and how to stay confident and believe in myself. Writing a blog is a huge commitment and I noticed that the best bloggers added content on a weekly basis.

I needed to follow the same principle and so my simple list of twelve challenges to be accomplished in twelve months then became 52 challenges. I split each of them into weeks. This, of course, had a greater impact as I could divide a particular goal into even smaller, more attainable chunks. My month of 'exercising more' became four separate events—cycling, Wii, skipping and walking. I ended up doing more than I had originally expected and I looked forward to the next week's challenge.

By breaking down my goals into weekly challenges, I was able to see clearly what I needed to do to achieve that particular challenge. I didn't have to think about the big picture, only that single task.

Doing this challenge has forced me to be very spontaneous, I book myself on courses without a second thought and I sign up for any new opportunities, as I see them as a base for learning new skills and meeting new people. When I think about the people and organisations I have linked with over the year I feel so honoured and proud of my achievements.

If I hadn't signed up for a writing workshop I would never have met Stan Nicholls, bestselling fantasy author of the Orcs series. In fact I didn't just *meet* him, I sat next to him for an entire workshop and we are now friends on Facebook!

None of this would have been possible if I hadn't made that decision on New Year's Eve and followed it through.

HOW-TO...

I hope you have enjoyed reading about my journey. It has been an incredible twelve months and the next twelve are set to be just as amazing.

Completing this challenge changed my life and I hope you have found some inspiration within these pages to try a few of my challenges for yourself.

If you would like to take on the ultimate challenge and Change Your Life in a Year, then here are my top tips to help you achieve it:

- Write a list of what you want to achieve or tell someone—this confirms that you are serious about it.

- Concentrate on one challenge at a time so you don't feel overwhelmed and give up.

- Make just one change each week or take one action step. For example, if you want to lose weight then your first step would be to join a slimming group or buy a healthy eating recipe book. Take it one step at a time.

- Celebrate your accomplishments.

- There is no such thing as failure; if you have a set-back, learn from it and move on.

- Start a blog or a Facebook page to track your progress. Making changes in the public eye can keep you motivated and positive feedback leaves you feeling inspired.

- Follow the Motivate Me Blog for more inspiration at:

www.motivatemenow.co.uk

or 'like' the blog's Facebook fan page at

www.facebook.com/motivatemeblog

The most important lesson I learned this year was how easy it can be to:

'Dream it, Live it and Become it'.

Change Your Life in a Year = Mission Completed!

USEFUL LINKS

Zentangle
www.zentangle.com

Drinkaware
www.drinkaware.co.uk

Alcohol Concern
www.alcoholconcern.org

Alcoholics Anonymous
www.alcoholics-anonymous.org.uk

AAMET
www.aamet.org

Nicki Grice Blog
www.sunshinegirlnicola.blogspot.co.uk

How to Eat Loads and Stay Slim
www.howtoeatloadsandstayslim.com

NaNoWriMo
www.nanowrimo.org

Female Entrepreneur Association Interview
www.femaleentrepreneurassociation.com/2013/11/
building-a-holistic-health-business/

Michele Knight
www.micheleknight.com

Cottages 4 You
www.cottages4you.co.uk

Mumsnet
www.mumsnet.com

ACKNOWLEDGMENTS

I'd like to thank my three amazing children, your endless encouragement has been my lifeline. Your unwavering belief that I would complete my mission, kept me going through the crazy moments and the knee knocking trials. I love you all so much.

To my incredible parents who have taken this journey with me, you have celebrated the high points and been there to dust me down when I hit a low point—or a cargo net! You encouraged me at every stage and supported me through the year just as you have through my entire life—I love you both and continue to be inspired by your actions.

To my friends and clients. You have listened to my stories and even recommended challenges for me to complete, you became the voice of encouragement on my blog posts, providing motivational feedback when I needed it. You urged me to keep going and were anxious to hear how I survived each week. You are my inspiration.

A huge thank you to my editor, Sooz for her patience, professionalism and dedication to helping me bring this book to life. I promise to avoid numbers in the next book!

Finally, thank you to you, the reader, for picking up this book in the hope you will be entertained. I hope I lived up to your expectation.

Lightning Source UK Ltd.
Milton Keynes UK
UKHW010706020822
406728UK00001B/149

9 781947 727465